THE DARK TOWER AND OTHER RADIO SCRIPTS

THE DARK TOWER AND OTHER RADIO SCRIPTS

LOUIS MACNEICE

faber and faber

This edition first published in 2008
by Faber and Faber Ltd
3 Queen Square, London WC1N 3AU

Printed by CPI Antony Rowe, Eastbourne

A CIP record for this book is available from the British Library

ISBN 978-0-571-24341-9

CONTENTS

GENERAL INTRODUCTION

The interest shown in such few radio scripts as have been published (the most notable recent example being *The Rescue* by my friend Mr. Edward Sackville-West) has encouraged me to publish some more of my own. I do this not only because like all radio writers I feel frustrated each time a script has been broadcast but in the hope that a selection of dissimilar pieces may throw some light on the medium. I have chosen *The Dark Tower* because I think it the best radio script I have written; the others are included as fairly clear-cut examples—I would certainly not say models—of different types of programme. All of them seem to me worth reading.

Having in my Introduction to *Christopher Columbus* essayed a general exposition of radio-dramatic writing, I will not labour again those main points which I still consider valid, e.g. that 'the first virtue of a radio script is construction'. But I would like in some respects to correct myself. That the radio writer 'must move on a more or less primitive plane' is, I think now, an overstatement or at least misleadingly expressed. What the radio writer must do, if he hopes to win the freedom of the air, is to appeal *on one plane*—whatever he may be doing on the others—to the more primitive listener and to the more primitive elements in anyone; i.e. he must give them (what Shakespeare gave them) entertainment.[1]

In the same Introduction I wrote: 'As compared with most contemporary literature, the objective elements will preponderate over the subjective, statement over allusion, synthesis over analysis.' This again I want to qualify; the comparison with contemporary *literature* may have misled me. The 'psychological' novel, concerned chiefly with 'subjective' experiences, deals

[1] The reception of *The Dark Tower* supports this. Many listeners said that they enjoyed it, found it 'beautiful', 'exciting' etc.—but had 'no idea what it was about.' In fact they were caught by the 'story' but I flatter myself that, in passing, the story 'slipped over' some meaning on them.

largely in *oratio obliqua*; even that kind of *oratio recta* used to represent 'the stream of consciousness' is usually not much more than a shorthand for the page. But when no character can be presented except through spoken words, whether in dialogue or soliloquy, that very *spokenness* makes this distinction between subjective and objective futile. A character in a radio play, as in a stage play, may say things that actually he never would or could say—the author may be making him utter what is only known to his unconscious—but once he has said them, there they are! As objective as Ben Jonson's Humours are objective. To take an extreme example, Virginia Woolf's novel *The Waves* is often quoted as subjective writing *par excellence*; the characters, thinking in the first person, say things they never could have formulated, being even as small children endowed with the brilliant introspection and the sad philosophy of their creator. I am confident that this method, though probably not this application of it, would be feasible on the air. Listeners might not accept Virginia Woolf's long-windedness, her preciousness, the sameness of her characters, the lack of a 'story'—but that in no way proves them 'allergic' to subjectivity. Once your characters speak speakable lines—once, to use a horrible piece of jargon, the subjective is objectified—you can get away with anything *so long as you entertain*.

Similarly, the distinctions made in my quotation between statement and allusion and between synthesis and analysis are perhaps equally worthless. It would have been safer to say that in radio dialogue we need a number of things which *sound like* statements—but in spoken dialogue that goes without saying; no two people can keep up a conversation which is one *hundred* per cent surrealist. As for allusion, not only is it difficult in any context to make any statement which is not also an allusion, i.e. suggestive of something beyond its own definitive meaning, but in all *dramatic* writing a word, let alone a phrase, pulls more than its dictionary weight; the pun is only the crudest example of a procedure familiar to, though not of course formulated by, everyone. In characterisation equally, Mr. X, who may appear to be talking at random and naturalistically, can really be talking succinctly and also symbolically, revealing himself—or whatever else is meant to be revealed—by a process of implicit logic. 'Implicit' is here, as in other creative writing, a key-word. Even in the psychological novel, if it is a good one, the psychology is implicit; for explicit psychology we go to the textbooks. This is all I meant in subordinating analysis to synthesis—but this too could have gone without saying or at least I ought so to have expressed it as not to preclude 'psychological' characterisation from the sphere of radio drama.

But criticism comes after the event; it is no good talking about radio until you have experienced it. It may therefore be instructive if, dropping generalities, I make a short confession of my own experiences as listener, script-writer, and producer. Before I joined the B.B.C. I was, like most of the intelligentsia, prejudiced not only against that institution but against broadcasting in general; I rarely listened to anything except concerts and running commentaries on sports events. These latter, which gave me a pleasure distinct from that which lies in *seeing* a game or race, should have provided a hint of radio's possibilities; my prejudice, however, prevented me from exploring the possible pleasures in wireless plays and features. Since then I have listened to many examples of both and must confess that often they give me no pleasure at all—but this proves nothing; we have all met the same disappointment with books, plays, and films. What does prove a point to me is that *some* plays and features have excited, amused, moved me. So the wireless *can* be worth listening to. But next: is it worth writing for?

Many writers are deterred from radio drama by fear of the middlemen and by dislike of actors. They expect their work to be doctored from the start and travestied in the presentation (which has of course sometimes happened—as it has happened both on the stage and page). But while no production will ever seem perfect to the author, the questions are whether one can gamble on a reasonably good production and whether such a production is better than none. Your answers depend on whether you really have an itch for drama; if you have, you must want sooner or later to write dialogue to be spoken somewhere—and it is no more likely to be spoken badly on the air than anywhere else (the wireless lacks the body of the stage—but also some of its impurities). If *you* provide a good script, the odds are that it will gain by being broadcast; in fact, if it loses, while it may be the fault of the production, the more likely inference is that your script was not radiogenic (a handy word, though jargon). The predominance of adapted stage-plays in B.B.C. programmes has probably discouraged a number of writers, for many of these plays do lose on the air (at least as compared with the stage); few of them are radiogenic. Transposition from one medium to another is usually unfair to both. Which is why we must remember that the script-writer is a peculiar species.

The all-important difference between visual and non-visual drama, while discouraging some, may encourage others towards radio, for here and here alone can one listen to calculated speech divorced from all visual supports or interferences—even from a printed page. It would be a great pity if television were ever completely to supersede sound broadcasting as the talkies superseded the silent films. That cinema revolution was inevitable but through it we lost the unique pleasure of watching a story told visually, dispensing with people's voices. But sound alone is for most people more potent, more pregnant, more subtle, than pictures alone and for that reason—regardless of the material pros and cons of television—I hope that sound broadcasting will survive, dispensing with people's faces. As with many other media its narrow limits are also its virtue, while within those limits it can give us something unobtainable from print (though print of course will always retain its proper autonomy). When I first heard a piece, which I had written for broadcasting, broadcast, I was irritated by details of presentation but excited and delighted by the total effect (there was more to my script, I felt, than I myself had realised). The mere fact that one's words issue from other people's mouths, while gratifying no doubt to an author's vanity, is also a welcome release from his involuntary egotism. Most novelists and poets, I think, envy the playwright that specious present and that feeling of *sharedness* which are given to a play by every fresh production, just as they envy the painter as composer-executant the excitement of his manual craftsmanship and the immediate impact of his completed work (which also can be shared by several people at once). When you have written for the page, you do not see your readers reading you; which is just as well as you could never tell if in their heads they were 'hearing' you properly. But in broadcasting you can, given the right speakers, force your listeners at least to hear the words as they should. The point is that here we have a means by which written lines can emulate the impact of a stage or of a painting and give the writer that excitement of a sensuous experience simultaneously shared with many which is one of the joys of life. This pleasure in a thing-being-performed-and-shared, while obtainable in all sports and some of the arts, is sadly lacking in the world of literature today. It is a pleasure I have often received, though mixed at times with mortification, when hearing my own scripts broadcast. It is succeeded, as I said before, by a feeling of frustration—because it is 'over'; but in that it is not of course unusual.

I have stressed this fact of pleasure because some people assume that writing for the wireless must be hackwork. It often is—for the salaried script-writer because he must turn his hand to many things, some of them dull, for the occasional writer (less forgivably) when he deals with an uncongenial subject for money or writes badly because he is merely writing for money. But it often is not. Broadcasting is plastic; while it can ape the Press, it can also emulate the arts. Yes, people will say, that is theoretically true but in practice you will never get art—or anything like it—out of a large public institution, encumbered with administrators, which by its nature must play for safety and to the gallery. This is not the place to dispute this at length but I would maintain that in this country such an institution cannot be really authoritarian; with ingenuity and a little luck a creative person can persuade (or fool) at least some of the administrators some of the time.[1] And, thinking of the vexed question of commercial broadcasting, I would add that many of the more original programmes by my friends and myself (this book shows examples in *The Dark Tower* and the 'March Hare' scripts) would have been no more acceptable to sponsored radio than to the biggest and vulgarest profit-making film company. For its acceptance of such experiments I am very grateful to the B.B.C.

In this age of irreconcilable idioms I have often heard writers hankering for some sort of group life, a desire doomed to disappointment; the modern writer—at any rate the modern poet—is *ipso facto* a spiritual isolationist who will lose far more than he will gain by trying to pool his mentality with those of his colleagues. Thus of the several dozen poets whom I know there are very few with whom I would wish to discuss poetry and only, I think, one from whom I would often accept criticism. This solitude (which incidentally has nothing to do with the Ivory Tower; there are Group Towers too, remember) is *in our time* salutary—but here again we cannot but envy playwrights, actors or musical executants. And here again I for one have found this missing group experience, in a valid form, in radio. Radio writers and producers *can* talk shop together because their shop is not, as with poets, a complex of spiritual intimacies but a matter of craftsmanship. Though the poet of course is also—or should be—a craftsman, the lyrical poet's technique is—or

[1] I am not suggesting that, as things are, all our administrators need persuading or fooling.

should be—closely wedded to his unique personality and there is no more point in defending your own personality than in impugning your friend's. But radio craftsmanship, like stage craftsmanship, is something much less private; we are fully entitled to discuss whether dialogue rings true, whether the dramatic climax is dramatic, how well the whole thing works. This is refreshing for a writer.

The popular assumption that all radio professionals resemble civil servants (resting on that other assumption that civil servants are automata) is flatly untrue. The department to which, at the date of writing, I belong in the B.B.C., would compare very well for intelligence with almost any contemporary salon of literati; my radio colleagues would be found on the whole quicker-witted, more versatile, less egocentric, less conventional, more humane. But, apart from these relishes to discussion, the reason why we can work together enjoyably and effectively is that in every case our work must go through the same mill, i.e. into a microphone and out at the other end through a wireless set. This very simple physical fact is such a bond of union as is rare among creative writers, playwrights again excepted. For we share the excitements and anxieties of *the performance*. This is especially so if we are our own executants, i.e. writer-producers. There are obvious drawbacks to this combination of functions—Mr. A as writer may see so clearly what he means that Mr. A as producer will fail to notice when the meaning is not coming over—but it does put a writer more closely in touch with his work-in-performance than he can be anywhere else unless he is Mr. Noel Coward. We know what happens to a film script when the multitude of 'experts' gets hold of it. On the stage there is no such multitude but there still is considerable interference and few writers have the chance, the time, the knowledge, or the capacity, to become stage-producers. But radio production being comparatively simple, not a few writers can learn to handle it—at any rate well enough to gain more than they lose (this especially applies to 'experimental' scripts where the pioneer, though an amateur, has an advantage over the professional geographer).

The script itself, after all, is only half the battle and the writer who merely sends in a script and does not go near the studios is working largely in the dark; whereas a writer who produces his own scripts will cut his coat according to his cloth. Since I have been producing my own programmes, I find that I both avail myself of facilities which I previously overlooked and avoid awkwardnesses which I previously imposed on my producer. Thus an earlier version of *Sunbeams in his Hat*, entitled *Dr. Chekhov*, was so written as to be almost unproduceable in places[1] at least without the use of multiple studios, as I typically had not envisaged the studio set-up. When I came to rewrite it for my own production I eliminated these difficulties and in so doing found I had made the script not only more manageable but more compact, more lucid, more convincing. Similarly, as regards both music and actors, the writer-producer has the advantage of being able to decide at an early stage who is going to do what. Thus, when he has a composer to write special music, he can not only get this music to fit the script but adjust his script on occasion to fit the music. He also has the say in casting, which is especially important in broadcasting both because of the shortness of rehearsals and because of the microphone's transparency to anything ham or unintelligent. In writing my more recent scripts I have always had an eye on the kinds of actor available and so avoided demanding the impossible and, when I could, the improbable; sometimes I have, from its conception, written a part for a particular actor, e.g. the Soldier in *The Nosebag* for Roy Emerton and the March Hare for Esmé Percy.

The preceding paragraph was intended to amplify my point about work-in-performance. While it is obviously not normally feasible for 'outside writers' to produce their own work, it is

[1] For which I now apologise to Mr. Stephen Potter—who in producing it saved the situation.

desirable, if not necessary, that they should be studio-minded; then they can explain to their producer what they want done without being embarrassing or nonsensical. I would like finally, since the chief object of this introduction was to disprove the assumption that broadcasting is 'inhuman', to inform my readers that every transmission of a play or feature, however unimportant the programme, should have—and usually has—the feeling of a First Night; it is something *being made* by a team of people.

For each of the scripts in this book I have written a separate introduction; but they all have this in common that, whatever my sins in either respect, I enjoyed both writing and producing them. The programme on Tchehov was suggested to me by my employers but the others I proposed myself. This gives me the opportunity of expressing my gratitude to the head of my department, Mr. Laurence Gilliam, who is as willing to accept such spontaneous suggestions as he is to allow an elastic treatment of those other programmes which 'have to be done'.

NOTES

The dialogue in these scripts is as broadcast but the directions have been re-written and considerably amplified.

The foregoing Introduction was written before the B.B.C. 'Third Programme' came into being. This new programme—for the first time, I believe, in radio history—assumes that its audience is going to *work* at its listening. So there is less question than ever of playing 'for safety and to the gallery'.

THE DARK TOWER

a radio parable play

TO

BENJAMIN BRITTEN

CAST

The Dark Tower was first broadcast in the B.B.C. Home Service on January 21st, 1946. The main parts, in order of their appearance, were played as follows:

SERGEANT-TRUMPETER	HARRY HUTCHINSON*
GAVIN	FRANK PARTINGTON*
ROLAND	CYRIL CUSACK
MOTHER	OLGA LINDO
TUTOR	MARK DIGNAM
SYLVIE	LUCILLE LISLE*
BLIND PETER	IVOR BARNARD
SOAK	ROBERT FARQUHARSON
STEWARD	HOWARD MARION-CRAWFORD
NEAERA	VERA MAXIME
SHIP'S OFFICER	CHARLES MAUNSELL*
PRIEST	ALEXANDER SARNER*
ROLAND'S FATHER	LAIDMAN BROWNE*
PARROT	MARJORIE WESTBURY*
RAVEN	STANLEY GROOME*
CLOCK VOICE	DUNCAN MCINTYRE*

Special music was composed by Benjamin Britten and conducted by Walter Goehr.

The production was by the author.

* A star denotes membership of the B.B.C. Repertory Company at the time of the broadcast. It will be seen from this and the other lists of cast in the book how useful this institution is.

INTRODUCTORY NOTE

The Dark Tower is a parable play, belonging to that wide class of writings which includes *Everyman*, *The Faerie Queene* and *The Pilgrim's Progress*. Though under the name of allegory this kind of writing is sometimes dismissed as outmoded, the clothed as distinct from the naked allegory is in fact very much alive. Obvious examples are *Peer Gynt* and the stories of Kafka but also in such books as *The Magic Mountain* by Thomas Mann, where the disguise of 'realism' is maintained and nothing happens that is quite inconceivable in life, it is still the symbolic core which makes the work important. My own impression is that pure 'realism' is in our time almost played out, though most works of fiction of course will remain realistic *on the surface*. The single-track mind and the single-plane novel or play are almost bound to falsify the world in which we live. The fact that there is method in madness and the fact that there is fact in fantasy (and equally fantasy in 'fact') have been brought home to us not only by Freud and other psychologists but by events themselves. This being so, reportage can no longer masquerade as art. So the novelist, abandoning the 'straight' method of photography, is likely to resort once more not only to the twist of plot but to all kinds of other twists which may help him to do justice to the world's complexity. Some element of parable therefore, far from making a work thinner and more abstract, ought to make it more concrete. Man does after all live by symbols.

The dual-plane work will not normally be allegory in the algebraic sense; i.e. it will not be desirable or even possible to equate each of the outward and visible signs with a precise or rational inner meaning. Thus *The Dark Tower* was suggested to me by Browning's poem 'Childe Roland to the Dark Tower came', a work which does not admit of a completely rational analysis and still less adds up to any clear moral or message. This poem has the solidity of a dream; the writer of such a poem, though he may be aware of the 'meanings' implicit in his dream, must not take the dream to pieces, must present his characters concretely, must allow the story to persist as a story and not dwindle into a diagram. While I could therefore have offered here an explicit summary of those implicit 'meanings' in *The Dark Tower* of which I myself was conscious, I am not doing so, because it might impair the impact of the play. I would merely say—for the benefit of people like the *Daily Worker's* radio critic, who found the programme pointless and depressing—that in my opinion it is neither. *The Faerie Queene, The Pilgrim's Progress, Piers Plowman* and the early Moralities could not have been written by men without any beliefs. In an age which precludes the simple and militant faith of a Bunyan, belief (whether consciously formulated or not) still remains a *sine qua non* of the creative writer. I have my beliefs and they permeate *The Dark Tower*. But do not ask me what Ism it illustrates or what Solution it offers. You do not normally ask for such things in the single-plane work; why should they be forced upon something much more complex? 'Why, look you now, how unworthy a thing you make of me!' What is life *useful* for anyway?

Comments on points of detail will be found at the end of this book. The best in this kind are but shadows—and in print they are shadows of shadows. To help the reader to *hear* this piece, I will therefore add this: in production I got the actors to play their parts 'straight', i.e. like flesh and blood (in dreams the characters are usually like flesh and blood too). Out of an excellent cast I am particularly grateful to Cyril Cusack for his most sensitive rendering of 'Roland'. And Benjamin Britten provided this programme with music which is, I think, the best I have heard in a radio play. Without his music *The Dark Tower* lacks a dimension.

THE DARK TOWER

OPENING ANNOUNCEMENT

The Dark Tower. The programme which follows is a parable play—suggested by Robert Browning's poem 'Childe Roland to the Dark Tower came'. The theme is the ancient but ever-green theme of the Quest—the dedicated adventure; the manner of presentation is that of a dream—but a dream that is full of meaning. Browning's poem ends with a challenge blown on a trumpet:

'And yet
Dauntless the slughorn to my lips I set
And blew. "Childe Roland to the Dark Tower came".'

Note well the words 'And yet'. *Roland did not have to—he did not wish to—and yet in the end he came to: The Dark Tower.*

(*A trumpet plays through the Challenge Call.*)

SERGEANT-TRUMPETER.
There now, that's the challenge. And mark this:
Always hold the note at the end.

GAVIN. Yes, Sergeant-Trumpeter, yes.

ROLAND (*as a boy*).
Why need Gavin hold the note at the end?

SERGEANT-TRUMPETER.
Ach, ye're too young to know. It's all tradition.

ROLAND. What's tradition, Sergeant-Trumpeter?

GAVIN. Ask Mother that one (*with a half-laugh*). She knows.

SERGEANT-TRUMPETER.
Aye, *she* knows.
But run along, sonny. Leave your brother to practise.
(*The trumpet begins—but breaks off.*)

SERGEANT-TRUMPETER.
No. Again.
(*The trumpet re-begins—breaks off.*)

SERGEANT-TRUMPETER.
Again.
(The trumpet re-begins and is sustained.)

SERGEANT-TRUMPETER.
That's it now. But hold that last note—hold it!
(On the long last note the trumpet fades into the distance.)

ROLAND. Mother! What's tradition?

MOTHER. Hand me that album. No—the black one.

ROLAND. Not the locked one!

MOTHER. Yes, the locked one. I have the key.
Now, Roland, sit here by me on the sofa.
We'll look at them backwards.

ROLAND. Why must we look at them backwards?

MOTHER. Because then you may recognise—
Now! You know who this is?

ROLAND. Why, that's my brother Michael.
And here's my brother Henry!
Michael and Henry and Denis and Roger and John!
(He speaks with the bright callousness of children.)
Do you keep this album locked because they're dead?

MOTHER. No . . . not exactly.
Now—can you guess who this is?

ROLAND. That's someone I saw in a dream once.

MOTHER. It must have been in a dream.
He left this house three months before you were born.

ROLAND. Is it . . . is it my father?

MOTHER. Yes. And this is your grandfather. And this is *his* father—
For the time being you needn't look at the rest;
This book goes back through seven long generations
As far as George the founder of the family.

ROLAND. And did they all die the same way?

MOTHER. They did, Roland. And now I've answered your question.

ROLAND (*already forgetting*).
What question, Mother?
(*The trumpet call is heard in the distance.*)

ROLAND. Ah, there's Gavin practising.
He's got it right at last.
(*The Call ends and Gavin appears.*)

GAVIN (*excited*).
Mother! I know the challenge. When can I leave? Tomorrow?

MOTHER. Why not today, Gavin?

GAVIN. Today! But I haven't yet checked my equipment;
I mean—for such a long journey I—

MOTHER. You will travel light, my son.

GAVIN. Well, yes . . . of course . . . today then.

ROLAND. Where are you going, Gavin?

GAVIN. Why, surely you know; I'm—

MOTHER. Hsh!

ROLAND. I know where he's going. Across the sea like Michael.

GAVIN. That's right, Roland. Across the big, bad sea.
Like Michael and Henry and Denis and Roger and John.
And after that through the Forest.
And after that through the Desert—

ROLAND. What's the Desert made of?

GAVIN. Well . . . I've never been there.
Some deserts are made of sand and some are made of grit but—

MOTHER (*as if to herself*).
This one is made of doubts and dried-up hopes.

ROLAND (*still bright*).
And what do you find at the other end of the desert?

GAVIN. Well, I . . . well . . .

MOTHER. You can tell him.

GAVIN. I find the Dark Tower.

(*The Dark Tower theme gives a musical transition to the schoolroom.*)

TUTOR. Now, Master Roland, as this is our first day of lessons
I trust I shall find you as willing a pupil
As your six brothers before you.

ROLAND. Did you like teaching my brothers?

TUTOR. Like it? It was an honour.
It was teaching to some purpose.

ROLAND. When's my brother Gavin coming back?

TUTOR. What!

ROLAND. Gavin. When's he coming back?

TUTOR. Roland! . . .
I see I must start from the beginning.
I thought your mother'd have told you but maybe being the youngest—

ROLAND. What would my mother have told me?

TUTOR. You ask when your brother Gavin is coming back?
You must get this straight from the start:
Your family never come back.
(*Roland begins to interrupt.*)

TUTOR. Now, now, now, don't let me scare you.
Sit down on that stool and I'll try to explain.
Now, Roland—
I said that to teach your brothers was an honour.
Before your mother engaged me to tutor John
I was an usher in a great city,
I taught two dozen lads in a class—
The sons of careerists—salesmen, middlemen, half-men,
Governed by greed and caution; it was my job
To teach them enough—and only enough—
To fit them for making money. Means to a means.
But with your family it is a means to an end.

ROLAND (*naïvely puzzled*).
My family don't make money?

TUTOR. They make history.

ROLAND. And what do you mean by an end?

TUTOR. I mean—surely they told you?
I mean: the Dark Tower.

ROLAND. Will *I* ever go to the Dark Tower?

TUTOR. Of course you will. That is why I am here.

ROLAND (*gaily*).
Oh well! That's different!

TUTOR. It is.

ROLAND. And that means I'll fight the Dragon?

TUTOR. Yes—but let me tell you:
We call it the Dragon for short, it is a nameless force
Hard to define—for no one who has seen it,
Apart from those who have seen its handiwork,
Has returned to give an account of it.
All that we know is there is something there
Which makes the Dark Tower dark and is the source
Of evil through the world. It is immortal
But men must try to kill it—and keep on trying
So long as we would be human.

ROLAND. What would happen
If we just let it alone?

TUTOR. Well . . . some of us would live longer; all of us
Would lead a degraded life, for the Dragon would be supreme
Over our minds as well as our bodies. Gavin—
And Michael and Henry and Denis and Roger and John—
Might still be here—perhaps your father too,
He would be seventy-five—but mark this well:
They would not be themselves. Do you understand?

ROLAND. I'm not quite sure, I . . .

TUTOR. You are still small. We'll talk of the Dragon later.
Now come to the blackboard and we'll try some Latin.

You see this sentence?

ROLAND. Per ardúa . . .

TUTOR. Per ardua ad astra.

ROLAND. What does it mean?

TUTOR. It does not go very well in a modern language.
We had a word 'honour'—but it is obsolete.
Try the word 'duty'; and there's another word—
'Necessity'.

ROLAND. Necessity! That's a bit hard to spell.

TUTOR. You'll have to spell it, I fear. Repeat this after me:
N—

ROLAND. N—

TUTOR. E—

ROLAND. E—

(*As they spell it through, their voices dwindle away and a tolling bell grows up out of the distance.*)

SERGEANT-TRUMPETER.
Ah God, there's the bell for Gavin.
He had the greatest power to his lungs of the lot of them.
And now he's another name in the roll of honour
Where Michael's is still new gold. Five years it is—
Or would it be more like six—since we tolled for Michael?
Bells and trumpets, trumpets and bells,
I'll have to be learning the young one next;
Then he'll be away too and my lady will have no more.

MOTHER (*coldly; she has come up behind him*).
No more children, Sergeant-Trumpeter?

SERGEANT-TRUMPETER.
Ach, I beg your pardon. I didn't see you.

MOTHER. No matter. But know this:
I have one more child to bear.
No, I'm not mad; you needn't stare at me, Sergeant.

This is a child of stone.

SERGEANT-TRUMPETER.
A child of . . . ?

MOTHER. Stone. To be born on my death-bed.
No matter. I'm speaking in metaphor.

SERGEANT-TRUMPETER (*relieved to change the subject*).
That's all right then. How's young Roland
Making out at his lessons?

MOTHER. I don't know. Roland lacks concentration; he's not like my other sons,
He's almost flippant, he's always asking questions—

SERGEANT-TRUMPETER.
Ach, he's young yet.

MOTHER. Gavin was his age once.
So were Michael and Henry and Denis and Roger and John.
They never forgot what they learnt. And they asked no questions.

SERGEANT-TRUMPETER.
Ah well—by the time that Roland comes to me
When he's had his fill of theory and is all set for action,
In another half dozen years when he comes to learn the trumpet call—

MOTHER. Hsh, don't talk of it now.
(*as if to herself*).
Let one bell toll at a time.

(*The bell recedes into nothing, covering a passage of years. Roland is now grown up.*)

TUTOR. So ends our course on ethics. Thank you, Roland;
After all these years our syllabus is concluded.
You have a brain; what remains to be tried is your will.
Remember our point today: the sensitive man
Is the more exposed to seduction. In six years

I have come to know you; you have a warm heart—
It is perhaps too warm for a man with your commission,
Therefore be careful. Keep to your one resolve,
Your single code of conduct, listen to no one
Who doubts your values—and above all, Roland,
Never fall in love—That is not for you.
If ever a hint of love should enter your heart,
You must arise and go . . . . That's it: Go!
Yes, Roland my son. Go quickly.

(*His last words fade slightly and Sylvie's voice fades in.*)

SYLVIE. But why must you go so quickly? Now that the sun's come out.

ROLAND. I have my lesson to learn.

SYLVIE. You're always learning lessons!
I'll begin to think you prefer your books to me.

ROLAND. Oh, but Sylvie, this isn't books any more.

SYLVIE. Not books? Then—

ROLAND. I'm learning to play the trumpet.

SYLVIE (*irritated*).
Whatever for? Roland, you make me laugh.
Is this another idea of your mother's?
I needn't ask. What's all this leading to?

ROLAND (*quietly*).
I could tell you, darling. But not today.
Today is a thing in itself—apart from the future.
Whatever follows, I will remember this tree
With this dazzle of sun and shadow—and I will remember
The mayflies jigging above us in the delight
Of the dying instant—and I'll remember *you*
With the bronze lights in your hair.

SYLVIE. Yes, darling; but why so sad?
There will be other trees and—

ROLAND. Each tree is itself, each moment is itself,
Inviolable gifts of time . . . of God—
But you cannot take them with you.

SYLVIE. Take them with you where?

ROLAND. Kiss me, Sylvie. I'm keeping my teacher waiting.
(*The Challenge Call is played through once.*)

SERGEANT-TRUMPETER.
Nicely blown! Nicely blown!
You've graduated, my lad.
But remember—when I'm not here—hold the note at the end.

ROLAND. (*a shade bitter*).
You mean when *I'm* not here.

SERGEANT-TRUMPETER.
Aye, you're right. But you are my last pupil,
I'll be shutting up shop, I want you to do me credit.
When you've crossed the sea and the desert and come to the place itself
I want you to do me credit when you unsling that horn.

ROLAND. I hope I will.
(*He pauses; then slightly embarrassed.*)

ROLAND. Sergeant?

SERGEANT-TRUMPETER.
Eh?

ROLAND. Do you believe in all this?

SERGEANT-TRUMPETER.
All what?

ROLAND. Do you think that there really is any dragon to fight?

SERGEANT-TRUMPETER.
What are you saying! What was it killed Gavin?
And Michael and Henry and Denis and Roger and John,
And your father himself and his father before him and all of them back to George!

ROLAND. I don't know but . . . nobody's *seen* this dragon.

SERGEANT-TRUMPETER.

Seen him? They've seen what he's done!
Have you never talked to Blind Peter?
I thought not. Cooped up here in the castle—
Inside this big black ring of smothering yew-trees—
You never mixed with the folk.
But before you leave—if you want a reason for leaving—
I recommend that you pay a call on Peter.
And his house is low; mind your head as you enter.

(*Another verbal transition.*)

BLIND PETER (*old and broken*).

That's right, sir; mind your head as you enter.
Now take that chair, it's the only one with springs,
I saved it from my hey-day. Well now, sir,
It's kind of you to visit me. I can tell
By your voice alone that you're your father's son;
Your handshake's not so strong though.

ROLAND. Why, was my father—

BLIND PETER.

He had a grip of iron.
And what's more, sir, he had a will of iron.
And what's still more again, he had a conscience—
Which is something we all need. *I* should know!

ROLAND. Why?

BLIND PETER.

Why what?

ROLAND. Why do you sound so sad when you talk about having a conscience?

BLIND PETER.

Because his conscience is something a man can lose.
It's cold in here, I'll make a long story short.
Fifty years ago when I had my sight—

But the Dragon was loose at the time—
I had a job and a wife and a new-born child
And I believed in God. Until one day—
I told you the Dragon was loose at the time,
No one had challenged him lately; so he came out from his den—
What some people call the Tower—and creeping around
He got to our part of the world; nobody saw him of course,
There was just like a kind of a bad smell in the air
And everything went sour; people's mouths and eyes
Changed their look overnight—and the government changed too—
And as for me I woke up feeling different
And when I looked in the mirror that first morning
The mirror said 'Informer'!

ROLAND (*startled*).

Informer?

BLIND PETER.

Yes, sir. My new rôle.
They passed a pack of laws forbidding this and that
And anyone breaking 'em—the penalty was death.
I grew quite rich sending men to their death.
The last I sent was my wife's father.

ROLAND. But . . . but did you believe in these laws?

BLIND PETER.

Believe? Aha! Did I believe in anything?
God had gone round the corner. I was acquiring riches.
But to make a long story short—
When they hanged my wife's father my wife took poison,
So I was left with the child. Then the child took ill—

Scared me stiff—so I sent for all the doctors,
I could afford 'em then—but they couldn't discover
Anything wrong in its body, it was more as if its soul
Was set on quitting—and indeed why not?
To be a human being, people agree, is difficult.

ROLAND. Then the child . . . ?

BLIND PETER.

Quit.
Yes; she quit—but slowly.
I watched it happen. That's why now I'm blind.

ROLAND. Why? You don't mean you yourself—

BLIND PETER.

When you've seen certain things, you don't want to see no more.
Tell me, sir. Are people's faces nowadays
As ugly as they were? You know what I mean: evil?

ROLAND. No, not most of them. *Some*, I suppose—

BLIND PETER.

Those ones belong to the Dragon.

ROLAND (*exasperated*).

Why put the blame of everything on the Dragon?
Men have free choice, haven't they?
Free choice of good or evil—

BLIND PETER.

That's just it—
And the evil choice is the Dragon!
But I needn't explain it to you, sir; *you've* made up your mind,
You're like your father—one of the dedicated
Whose life is a quest, whose death is a victory.
Yes! God bless you! *You've* made up your mind!

ROLAND (*slowly and contemplatively*).

But have I, Peter? Have I?

(*Verbal transition.*)

SYLVIE. Have you, Roland dearest? Really made up your mind?

ROLAND (*without expression*).
I go away today.

SYLVIE. That's no answer.
You go away because they tell you to.
Because your mother's brought you up on nothing
But out of date beliefs and mock heroics.
It's easy enough for her—

ROLAND (*indignantly*).
Easy for her?
Who's given her flesh and blood—and I'm the seventh son!

SYLVIE. I've heard all that. They call it sacrifice
But each new death is a stone in a necklace to her.
Your mother, Roland, is mad.

ROLAND (*with quiet conviction*).
The world is mad.

SYLVIE. Not all of it, my love. Those who have power
Are mad enough but there *are* people, Roland,
Who keep themselves to themselves or rather to each other,
Living a sane and gentle life in a forest nook or a hill pocket,
Perpetuating their kind and their kindness, keeping
Their hands clean and their eyes keen, at one with
Themselves, each other and nature. I had thought
That you and I perhaps—

ROLAND. There is no perhaps
In my tradition, Sylvie.

SYLVIE. You mean in your family's.
Isn't it time you saw that you were different?
You're no knight errant, Roland.

ROLAND. No, I'm not.
But there is a word 'Necessity'—

SYLVIE. Necessity? You mean your mother's orders.

ROLAND (*controlled*).
Not quite. But apart from that,
I saw a man today—they call him Blind Peter—

SYLVIE. Leave the blind to mislead the blind. That Peter
Is where he is because of his own weakness;
You can't help him, Roland.

ROLAND. Maybe not—
(*with sudden insight*).
But maybe I can do something to prevent
A recurrence of Blind Peters.

SYLVIE. Imagination!

ROLAND. Imagination? . . . That things can be bettered?
That action can be worth-while? That there are ends
Which, even if not reached, are worth approaching?
Imagination? Yes, I wish I had it—
I have a little—You should support that little
And not support my doubts.

(*A drum-roll is heard.*)

ROLAND. Listen; there is the drum.
They are waiting for me at the gate.
Sylvie, I—

SYLVIE. Kiss me at least.

(*Pause, while the drum changes rhythm.*)

ROLAND. I shall never—

SYLVIE. See me again?
You will, Roland, you will.
I know you. You will set out but you won't go on,
Your common sense will triumph, you'll come back.
And your love for me will triumph and in the end—

ROLAND. This is the end. Goodbye.

(*The drum swells and ends on a peak. This is the Scene of Departure.*)

TUTOR. To you, Roland, my last message:
For seven years I have been your tutor.
You have worked hard on the whole but whether really
You have grasped the point of it all remains to be seen.
A man lives on a sliding staircase—
Sliding downwards, remember; to be a man
He has to climb against it, keeping level
Or even ascending slightly; he will not reach
The top—if there is a top—and when he dies
He will slump and go down regardless. All the same
While he lives he must climb. Remember that.
And I thank you for your attention. Goodbye, Roland.

SERGEANT-TRUMPETER.
To you, Roland, my last message:
You are off now on the Quest like your brothers before you
To take a slap at the Evil that never dies.
Well, here's this trumpet; sling it around your waist
And keep it bright and clean till the time comes
When you have to sound the challenge—the first and the last time—
And I trust you will do your old instructor credit
And put the fear of God—or of Man—into that Dragon.
That's all now. God bless you. But remember—
Hold that note at the end.

MOTHER. To you, Roland, my last message:
Here is a ring with a blood-red stone. So long as
This stone retains its colour, it means that I
Retain my purpose in sending you on the Quest.
I put it now on your finger.

ROLAND. Mother! It burns.

MOTHER. That is the heat in the stone. So long as the stone is red
The ring will burn and that small circle of fire
Around your little finger will be also
The circle of my will around your mind.
I gave a ring like this to your father, Roland,
And to John and Roger and Denis and Henry and Michael
And to Gavin the last before you. My will was around and behind them.
Should ever you doubt or waver, look at this ring—
And feel it burn—and go on.

ROLAND. Mother! Before I go—

MOTHER. No more words. Go!
Turn your face to the sea. (*Raising her voice.*) Open the gates there!
(*aside*) The March of Departure, Sergeant.
Let my son go out—my last. And make the music gay!

(*The March begins at full volume, then gradually dwindles as Roland and the listener move away. By the time the music has vanished Roland has reached the Port, where he addresses a stranger.*)

ROLAND. Forgive me stopping you, sir—

SOAK (*old, alcoholic, leering*).
Forgive you? Certainly not.
I'm on my way to the Tavern.

ROLAND. I'm on my way to the quays. Is it this turning or next?

SOAK. Any turning you like. Look down these stinking streets—
There's sea at the end of each of 'em.
Yes, young man, but what's at the end of the sea?
Never believe what they said when you booked your passage.

ROLAND. But I haven't booked it yet.

SOAK. Not booked your passage yet! Why, then there's no need to hurry.
You come with me to the Tavern; it's only a step.

ROLAND. I cannot spare a step.

SOAK. All right, all right;
If you won't come to the Tavern, the Tavern must come to you.
Ho there, music!

(*The orchestra strikes up raggedly—continuing while he speaks.*)

SOAK. That's the idea. Music does wonders, young man.
Music can build a palace, let alone a pub.
Come on, you masons of the Muses, swing it,
Fling me up four walls. Now, now, don't drop your tempo;
Easy with those hods. All right; four walls.
Now benches—tables—No! No doors or windows.
What drunk wants daylight? But you've left out the bar.
Come on—'Cellos! Percussion! All of you! A bar!
That's right. Dismiss!

(*The music ends.*)

SOAK. Barmaid.

BARMAID. Yes, sir?

SOAK. Give us whatever you have and make it triple.

ROLAND. Just a small one for me, please.

SOAK. Oh don't be so objective. One would think,
Looking at your long face, that there's a war on.

ROLAND. But—

SOAK. There is no war on—and you have no face.
Drink up. Don't be objective.

ROLAND. What in the name of—

BARMAID. Look, dearie; don't mind *him*.
He always talks like that. You take my tip;
You're new here and this town is a sea-port,
The tone is rather . . . . You go somewhere inland.

ROLAND. But how can I?
I have to go to sea.

BARMAID (*seriously*).
The sea out there leads nowhere.

SOAK. Come, sweetheart, the same again.

BARMAID. Nowhere, I've warned you. (*In a whisper.*) As for our friend here,
Don't stay too long in his company.

SOAK. What's that? Don't stay too long in my what?

BARMAID. Company was the word.

SOAK. Company? I have none. Why, how could I?
There's never anyone around where I am.
I exist for myself and all the rest is projection.
Come on, projection, drink! Dance on your strings and drink!

BARMAID. Oblige him, dearie, oblige him.

SOAK. There! My projection drinks.
I wrote this farce before I was born, you know—
This puppet play. In my mother's womb, dear boy—
I have never abdicated the life of the womb.
Watch, Mabel: my new puppet drinks again—
A pretty boy but I've given him no more lines.
Have I, young man?

(*pause*)

You see, he cannot speak.
All he can do henceforward is to drink—
Look! A pull on the wire—the elbow lifts.
Give him the same again.

BARMAID. Well . . . .

SOAK. There is no well about it. Except the well
That has no bottom and that fills the world.
Triplets, I said. Where are those damned musicians?
Buck up, you puppets! Play!

(*The orchestra strikes up a lullaby, continued behind his speech.*)

SOAK (*sleepily*).

Good. Serenade me now till I fall asleep
And all the notes are one—and all the sounds are silence.
Unity, Mabel, unity is my motto.
The end of drink is a whole without any parts—
A great black sponge of night that fills the world
And when you squeeze it, Mabel, it drips inwards.
D'you want me to squeeze it? Right. Piano there.
Piano—I must sleep. Didn't you hear me?
Piano, puppets. All right, pianissimo.
Nissimo . . . nissimo . . . issimo . . . .

(*The music ends and only his snoring is heard.*)

ROLAND. A puppet? . . . A projection? . . . How he lies!
And yet I've sometimes thought the same, you know—
The same but the other way round.
There is no evidence for anything
Except my own existence—he says his.
But he's wrong anyway—look at him snoring there.
If I were something existing in his mind
How could I go on now that he's asleep?

SOAK (*muffled*).

Because I'm dreaming you.

ROLAND. Dreaming?

BARMAID. Yes, sir.
He does have curious dreams.

SOAK. Yes, and the curious thing about my dreams
Is that they always have an unhappy ending
For all except the dreamer. Thus at the moment
You'd never guess, young man, what rôle I've cast you for—

ROLAND. What the—

BARMAID. Never mind, dear.

Tomorrow he'll wake up.

ROLAND. Tomorrow *he'll* wake up?
And I—Shall I wake up? Perhaps to find
That this whole Quest is a dream. Perhaps I'm still at home
In my bed by the window looking across the valley
Between the yew-trees to where Sylvie lives
Not among yews but apples—

(He is interrupted by a terrific voice crashing in on the 'Bar' from the outer world.)

STENTOR. All Aboard!

ROLAND. What's that?

STENTOR. All Aboard!

SOAK. You'd never guess
What happens in my dream . . . .

STENTOR. All Aboard! All Aboard!
Come along there, young man—unless you want to be left.
All Aboard for the Further Side of the Sea,
For the Dead End of the World and the Bourne of No Return!

(The noise of a crowd materialises, increasing.)

STENTOR. All Aboard, ladies and gents, knaves and fools, babes and sucklings,
Philistines, pharisees, parasites, pimps,
Nymphos and dipsos—All Aboard!
Lost souls and broken bodies; make it snappy.
That's right, folks. Mind your feet on the gangway.

(Through the racket of gadarening passengers is heard the mechanical voice of the Ticket Collector.)

TICKET COLLECTOR.
Ticket? Thank you . . . Ticket? Thank you . . . Ticket? Thank you . . . Ticket? Thank you . . . .

(The crowd noises fade out; Roland is now below decks.)

STEWARD (*with an 'off-straight' accent*).
This way, sir. Let me show you your stateroom.
Hot and cold and a blue light over the bed.
Ring once for a drink, twice for an aspirin.
Now if you want anything else—a manicure, for example—

ROLAND. No, steward. A sleeping draught.

STEWARD (*archly*).
Sir! In the morning?

ROLAND. Morning be damned. My head aches.

STEWARD. Drinking last night, sir?

ROLAND. Thinking.

STEWARD (*rattling it off*).
Thinking? That's too bad, sir.
But you'll soon get over that, sir.
In this ship nobody thinks, sir.
Why should they? They're at sea, sir . . .
And if your brain's at sea, sir—

ROLAND (*angrily*).
Listen! I want a sleeping draught.
How many times do I have to ring for that?

STEWARD (*unperturbed*).
As many times as you like, sir.
If you can keep awake, sir.
(*pimpishly*) But talking of sleeping draughts, sir,
Do you hear that lady playing the fiddle?

ROLAND. Fiddle? No. I don't.

STEWARD. Ah, that's because she plays it in her head.
But she's a very nice lady, sir.
Her name, sir, is Neaera.

ROLAND. Why should I care what her name is?
I tell you, steward—

STEWARD. Of course if you'd rather play tombola—

ROLAND. Tombola?

STEWARD (*throwing it away*).

Game of chance, sir. They call out numbers.
Kills the time, sir. Rather like life, sir.
You can buy your tickets now in the lounge.
The ship's started, you know, sir.

ROLAND. Oh, so the ship's started?
(*worried*) But I can't hear the engines.

STEWARD. Can't you, sir? I was right then.

ROLAND. Right? What do you mean?

STEWARD. I thought so the moment I saw you.
You don't, sir; of course you don't.

ROLAND. Don't what, damn you? Don't what?

STEWARD. *You* don't know where you're going, sir.

(*The ship's engines are heard on the orchestra; from them emerges the chatter of the lounge with the banal laughter of tombola players.*)

OFFICER. Clickety-click; sixty-six . . .
Kelly's Eye: Number One . . .
And we—

CROWD (*raggedly*).

Shake the Bag!

(*The orchestral engines give place to a solo violin.*)

NEAERA (*to herself, velvety*).

. . . Andantino . . . rallentando . . . adagio—

(*Her violin-playing breaks off.*)

NEAERA (*foreign accent*).

Mon Dieu! You startled me.

ROLAND. I'm sorry, I—

NEAERA (*cooingly*).

Do sit down. So you're going Nowhere too?

ROLAND. On the contrary, Madam—

NEAERA. Call me Neaera.

ROLAND. But—

NEAERA. And I'll call you Roland.

ROLAND. How do you know my name?

NEAERA. A little bird told me. A swan, if you want to know;
He sang your name and he died.
That's right, sit down. I've seen your dossier too.

ROLAND. Seen my—

NEAERA. Oh yes, chéri. In the Captain's cabin.

ROLAND. But how can I have a dossier? I've done nothing.

NEAERA. That's just it. It's dull.
But the future part amuses me.
Oh yes, my dear, this dossier includes the future—
And you don't come out of it well.

ROLAND. What do you mean?

NEAERA. You never believed in this Quest of yours, you see—
The Dark Tower—the Dragon—all this blague.
That's why you were so easy to seduce
In the idle days at sea—the days that are just beginning.

(Her violin begins again, then gives way to the lounge chatter, covering a passage of time.)

OFFICER. Key of the Door: Twenty-One!
Eleventh Hour: Eleven!
Ten Commandments: Nine!
Kelly's Eye: Number One!
And we—

CROWD. Shake the Bag!

(The violin re-emerges.)

NEAERA. . . . Lento . . . accelerando . . . presto . . . calando . . . morendo . . . .

(The violin fades away; it is meant to have established an affaire between Roland and Neaera.)

STEWARD *(slyly)*.
Well, sir? So the lady is still practising.
Golden days, sir, golden days.
At sea, sir, have you noticed

One doesn't notice time?
You probably feel you just came on board yesterday
And yet you got your sea-legs weeks ago, sir.

ROLAND. Sea-legs? Why, this trip has been so calm
I've never felt—

STEWARD. That's right, sir; never feel.
There's nothing in life but profit and pleasure.
Allegro assai—some people plump for pleasure
But I now fancy the profit—

(*Receiving a tip.*)

Ah thank you, sir, thank you.
The sea today in the sun, sir, looks like what shall I say, sir?

ROLAND. The sea today? A dance of golden sovereigns.

NEAERA. The sea today is adagios of doves.

ROLAND. The sea today is gulls and dolphins.

NEAERA. The sea today is noughts and crosses.

OFFICER (*cutting in rapidly*).
And we—

CROWD. Shake the Bag!

NEAERA. The sea today, Roland, is crystal.

ROLAND. The sea today Neaera, is timeless.

NEAERA. The sea today is drums and fifes.

ROLAND. The sea today is broken bottles.

NEAERA. The sea today is snakes and ladders.

OFFICER (*as before*).
Especially snakes!

CROWD. Especially snakes!

NEAERA (*wheedling*).
Roland, what's that ring? I've never seen one like it.

ROLAND. There is no other ring like it.

NEAERA. A strange ring for a man . . .
My colour, you know—that red . . .
Why do you twitch your finger?

ROLAND. Because it burns.

NEAERA. It burns?
Like tingling ears perhaps? Someone is thinking of you.

ROLAND (*startled—and suddenly depressed*).
What? . . . I hope not.
(*changing the subject*)
Come, darling, let's have a drink.

OFFICER. And we—

CROWD. Shake the Bag!

ROLAND. The sea today is drunken marble.

NEAERA. The sea today is silver stallions.

ROLAND. The sea today is—Tell me, steward:
Where's all this floating seaweed come from?

STEWARD. I imagine, sir—forgive me mentioning it—
That we are approaching land.

ROLAND. Land!

STEWARD. Yes, sir—but *you* won't be landing of course.
The best people never land, sir.

ROLAND. No? . . . (*to himself, fatalistically*) I suppose not.

(*Neaera's violin is heard again.*)

NEAERA (*to herself*).
. . . piu sonoro . . . con forza . . . accelerando . . . crescendo . . . .

(*The orchestra is added for a final crashing chord and at once we hear the hubbub of a crowd.*)

STENTOR. Anyone more for the shore? Anyone more for the shore?
Line up there on the forward deck
All what wants to chance their neck!
Anyone more for the shore?

TICKET COLLECTOR.
This way: thank you—This way: thank you—
This way: thank you—This way: thank you.

STENTOR. Anyone more? Hurry up please!
But remember this: Once you're off
You can't come back not ever on board.
We leave at once. At once!

TICKET COLLECTOR.
This way: thank you—This way: thank you—This way: thank you—This way: thank you.

1ST PASSENGER (*cockney*).
Here, here, who're you shoving? What's the blinkin' hurry?

HIS WIFE. That's right.

1ST PASSENGER.
Some people seem very keen to land in the future.
Can't use their eyes—if you ask me!

HIS WIFE. That's right. Look at them vicious rocks.

1ST PASSENGER.
And that tumble-down shack what thinks it's a Customs House.

HIS WIFE. And them horrible mountains behind it.

2ND PASSENGER (*northern*).
You'd think this country was uninhabited.

TICKET COLLECTOR.
This way: thank you—This way: thank you— (*with finality*) This way: thank *you*!
(*wearily*) O.K., sir. That's the lot.

STENTOR. Gangway up! Gangway up!
Clear away there. Mind your heads!

NEAERA. What are you staring at, Roland?
Come away, chéri; the show's over.
There goes the gangway; we're moving out now.
What *are* you staring at, darling?

ROLAND (*to himself*).
Was that . . . was that . . . I couldn't see in the face of the sun but—

Steward, you've sharp eyes.
Did you see over there on the quay, sitting on a rusty bollard—

STEWARD. Hsh, sir, Neaera will hear you.
Yes, sir; a very nice piece.
She was looking at you, sir, too—staring in fact, one might say.
Seems to be staring still—but what's she doing now?
Climbing up on the bollard?
Good Lord, sir, that's bad form; she's making gestures.

SYLVIE (*distant cry*).
Roland! . . . Roland! . . .

ROLAND. Sylvie!
I knew it. Out of my way there!

STENTOR. Here, here, here! Stop him!
Man gone mad there! Don't let him jump!

(*General commotion.*)

NEAERA. Roland! Come back!

(*A loud splash from the orchestra.*)

STENTOR. Man overboard! Man overboard!

(*The crowd reacts excitedly.*)

STENTOR. Lifebuoy! Where's the lifebuoy?

VOICE. Garn! This here ship don't carry no lifebuoys.
Nor he won't need one. Look! He's climbing up on the quay.

(*The orchestral engines start up again.*)

OFFICER (*triumphantly*).
And we—

CROWD. Shake the Bag!

NEAERA (*now revealing her hardness*).
Well, James . . . That's that.

STEWARD. Yes, madam.

NEAERA. You can drop the madam now.

STEWARD. Yes, Neaera—my sweetie-pie.

NEAERA (*matter-of-fact*).

That's more like it, James, my great big he-man.
Come to my cabin now; we'll count the takings.

(*The fading engines take the liner to sea; Roland is left on the Shore, with Sylvie sobbing.*)

ROLAND (*dead-pan*).

There she goes now.

SYLVIE (*echoing him*).

There she goes now . . . .

(*then bursting out*)

Roland, you are a hypocrite!

ROLAND (*quietly—but ashamed*).

No, Sylvie; merely a sleep-walker.
Ugh! (*He shivers.*)

SYLVIE (*calm again*).

The sea must have been cold. Come, let's walk.

ROLAND. How did you get here, Sylvie?

SYLVIE (*a shade bitter*).

I followed you—but not on a luxury liner.
Mine was a cargo boat, its limit was seven knots.

ROLAND. And yet you got here first.
And now I suppose you regret it.
Are you going to leave me, Sylvie?

SYLVIE. How can I? We're marooned here.
This is a desolate land. (*With forced control*) I suggest we keep together.

ROLAND. You have the gift of forgiveness.

SYLVIE. I have the gift of common sense.
As you're bound to be seduced from your so-called Quest,
In future, Roland, leave the seducing to me.
Or can't I, perhaps, compete with your ladies of pleasure?

ROLAND. Pleasure? That was not pleasure.

SYLVIE. It was. But it was not happiness.

ROLAND. And *you* offer me happiness?

SYLVIE. You doubt that I have it to offer?

ROLAND. No, I don't doubt that. But my tutor always said
Happiness cannot be taken as a present.

SYLVIE. Forget your tutor. This is a foreign land
Where no one will interfere with us.

ROLAND. No one? No *man* perhaps.

SYLVIE. What do you mean by that?

ROLAND. Look round you, Sylvie. See the deserted port,
The ruined shacks, the slag-heaps covered with lichen
And behind it all the frown and fear of the forest.
This is the Dragon's demesne.

SYLVIE. Roland, how childish you are.

ROLAND. You think so? Look at this notice
That flaps here on the hoarding—
And this one and this one and this one.

SYLVIE (*reading*).
'Wanted for Murder' . . . 'Wanted for Murder' . . .
'Wanted'—

ROLAND. You're reading the words wrong. Not 'for', Sylvie; 'to!'

SYLVIE. 'Wanted to Murder'. You're right.
But what does it mean?

ROLAND. It means we are on a soil where murder pays.

SYLVIE. It pays in many places.

ROLAND. Yes, but here
The paymaster is the government—and pay-day
Is every day of the week.
The Dragon's doing, I tell you.

SYLVIE. Well, if it is, *you* cannot cure it.
At the best you can cure yourself—
(*tentatively*) And that only through love.

ROLAND. Love?

SYLVIE (*stronger*).

Through me, Roland, through me.

(*pause*)

ROLAND (*quietly, as if solving a problem*).

Yes, I think you're right.

(*Then with sudden decisiveness*)

Sylvie, take this ring; I cannot wear it now,
I have failed this ring—but this ring will not fail you.

SYLVIE. You mean . . . ?

ROLAND. Yes. Let me put it on your finger.

SYLVIE. Not yet, Roland. That must be done in a church.

ROLAND. And where can we find a church round here?

SYLVIE (*half abstracted*).

What a strange colour. Like the blood of a child.

ROLAND. I repeat! Where can we find a church or a chapel here?

(*The Tout pops up. He speaks in broken English.*)

TOUT. 'Scusa. Lady and gentleman want guide to chapel?

ROLAND. God! Where did this come from?

TOUT. Me? Me come from sewer.
Me accredited guide—very good, very funny.
Lady and gentleman see chapel today?

ROLAND. Where is this chapel of yours?

TOUT. Chapel not mine, chapel belong to God.
Me take you there up this road, see.
Me tell you history, very much history, cheap.

(*A distant bell is heard, which continues as they speak.*)

TOUT. That chapel bell, tee-hee!
Ting-a-ling for the wedding!

ROLAND. What wedding?

TOUT. Me not know. No, sir, nobody know.
Happy pair not come yet.

SYLVIE. Roland, this is a sign.
Tell him to show us the way.

TOUT. Me show you the way sure.
Beautiful lady put best foot first.
Chapel up there in forest.

ROLAND. In the forest?

TOUT. Sure, boss. Chapel old.
Chapel in forest before forest grew.
But needs repairs now bad.
Haunted too—tee-hee!

ROLAND. Haunted!

TOUT. Sure, boss.
Plenty ghosts—tu-whit, tu-whoo.
Me need bonus for them ghosts.

ROLAND. You'll have your bonus. Only get us there quick.
Sylvie, we will exorcise these ghosts.
You know how, my dearest?

SYLVIE (*heart-felt*).
I know how.

(*The bell continues but is gradually submerged by orchestral chapel music. The latter swells to a definite close, leaving Roland and Sylvie in the Haunted Chapel. The voices echo in the emptiness.*)

PRIEST (*old and tired but kindly*).
You have the ring? Good.
Before I complete this ceremony making you man and wife
I must deliver a warning.
The original sin is doubt.
And in these days of contempt for the individual
It is also the topical sin.
So if either of you has doubts of the holiness of marriage
Or if either of you has doubts of the other
And can conceive a time when he or she
Will think again and wish this thing undone,
Now is your time to speak.

(*pause*)

Good. So you have no doubts. There is one other formality.
Although there is no congregation present,
Although apart from ourselves and a few sparrows and field-mice
This chapel is now empty, I must still put the question:
If anyone here know just cause or impediment—

(*He is interrupted by voices with a strange acoustic.*)

BLIND PETER'S VOICE.

I do!

GAVIN'S VOICE.

I do!

FATHER'S VOICE.

I do!

BLIND PETER'S VOICE.

This young man who's come to you to get married
Promised me when he left, a week before I died,
As he would avenge my blindness and bring it about
How no one should go the way I went in future.
Well, has he done it? No, and he'll never do it—
Not if you splice him up to that poor simple girl
Who only dreams how he and she will be happy.

GAVIN'S VOICE.

No, Roland, my brother; Blind Peter is right.
Forget your dreams of a home. You can never be happy
If you forsake the Quest. And if you could—
Happiness is not all. You must go on—
Turn your back on this chapel, go on through the forest,
Alone, always alone, and then across the desert,
And at the other end of that desert—

FATHER'S VOICE (*very deep*).

You will find what I found, Roland.

ROLAND. You?

FATHER'S VOICE.

You should know my voice though you never heard it.
Though you had not seen me, you knew my portrait.

ROLAND. My father?

FATHER'S VOICE.

I am still waiting to be your father.
While you malinger, you are no son of mine.

ROLAND (*shattered*).

Sylvie . . . .

SYLVIE. I know what you want . . . Your ring.

(*She tries to retain self-control in making her renunciation.*)

There . . . Back on your finger.
Look how it glows in this darkness.

ROLAND (*bitterly*).

Glows? It will burn me up.

SYLVIE. Roland, before we part—

PRIEST. This chapel is now closed. I am sorry.
Goodbye, my daughter; your way lies back,
Back by the road you came over the hopeless sea,
Back to your little house and your apple orchard
And there must you marry one of your own kind
And spray the trees in spring and raise the ladders in autumn
And spread the shining crop on the spare-room floor and—

ROLAND. Sylvie, before we part—

PRIEST. This chapel is now closed. I am sorry.
Goodbye, my son; your way lies forward,
Forward through the gibbering guile of the forest,
Forward through the silent doubt of the desert.
And here let me warn you: if in the forest

You hear any voices call from the trees,
Pay no attention, Roland, pay no attention . . . .

(His voice fades as forest music grows up; out of its tangle come the voices of the Birds, harsh and mechanical, speaking in a heavily stressed sing-song rhythm.)

PARROT. Pretty Polly! Pretty Polly!
Who's this coming now?

RAVEN. Caw-caw! Caw-caw!
Who's a-walkin' in *my* forest?

PARROT. Pretty Polly! The leaves have fallen.

RAVEN. Caw-caw! He's walking late.

PARROT. Pretty Polly! He's looking pale.

RAVEN. Caw-caw! His bones will be paler.

PARROT. Pretty Polly! Here he comes.

RAVEN. Caw-caw! Greet him!

PARROT *(sneeringly)*.
Where are you going, Roland, so fast?

RAVEN. Roland, running away from your past?

BOTH. You can't do *that*! You can't do *that*!

PARROT. Still on the road? Still on the Quest?

RAVEN. None achieve it but the best.

BOTH. You're not the sort. You're not the sort.

PARROT. Why not stop, my dear young man?

RAVEN. Let heroes die as heroes can.

BOTH. *You* must *live*! *You* must *live*!
(The forest music swells up as Roland passes.)

PARROT. Pretty Polly! He's passed us by.

RAVEN. Caw-caw! The devil take him.

PARROT. Pretty Polly! The devil will.

(The forest music gives place to desert music and Roland is heard soliloquising.)

ROLAND *(very tired)*.
Oh this desert!
The forest was bad enough but this beats all.

When my tutor described it to me, it sounded strange
But now I am here, with the grit of it filling my shoes,
I find that the worst thing about it is this:
The desert is something familiar.
And with no end—no end.

(*The music ends. A mechanical voice creeps in.*)

CLOCK VOICE.

Tick Tock, Tick Tock,
Sand and grit, bones and waste,
A million hours—all the same,
A million minutes—each an hour,
And nothing stops for nothing starts
But the hands move, the dead hands move,
The desert is the only clock—
Tick Tock, Tick Tock,
Tick Tock, Tick Tock . . . .

(*The Clock Voice recedes but can just be heard ticking as Roland speaks, with the Desert registering again musically.*)

ROLAND. Flat—No shape—No colour—Only here and there
A mirage of the past—something I've met before—
Figures arising from dust, repeating themselves,
Telling me things that I have no wish to remember.
Mirage . . . mirage . . . mirage . . . .

(*The music ends and the Clock comes near again.*)

CLOCK VOICE.

Tick Tock, Tick Tock,
Tick Tock, Tick Tock . . . .

(*continuing in the background as the first mirage is heard.*)

SOAK. A pretty boy—but I've given him no more lines.
He'd never guess what happens in my dream.
Look—a pull on the wire, his feet move forward.
Left Right, Left Right . . . .

(*He synchronises with the Clock Voice as it comes again into the foreground.*)

CLOCK VOICE. } Tick Tock etc.
SOAK. } Left Right etc.

(They withdraw to the background as the second mirage appears.)

STEWARD. Golden days, sir, golden days.
In the desert, sir, have you noticed
One doesn't notice time?
But I thought so the moment I saw you:
You don't know where you're going.
Golden days, golden days . . . .

(He synchronises with the Clock Voice and Soak—the same procedure.)

CLOCK VOICE. } Tick Tock, etc.
SOAK. } Left Right, etc.
STEWARD. } Golden days, etc.

NEAERA. . . . adagio . . . rallentando . . .
This dossier includes your future—
You don't come out of it well.
But kiss me, Roland, kiss me.
Kiss me, kiss me . . . .

(synchronises)

CLOCK VOICE. } Tick Tock, etc.
SOAK. } Left Right, etc.
STEWARD. } Golden days, etc.
NEAERA. } Kiss me, etc.

SYLVIE. But why must you go so quickly?
Now that the sun's come out.
You, Roland—you're no knight errant.
Your love for me will triumph, you'll come back,
Then you and I, you and I . . . .

(synchronises)

CLOCK VOICE. } Tick Tock, etc.
SOAK. } Left Right, etc.
STEWARD. } Golden days, etc.
NEAERA. } Kiss me, etc.
SYLVIE. } You and I, etc.

(The five voices swell in the foreground, driving as it were at the camera, till Roland can bear it no longer.)

ROLAND *(screaming)*.

NO!

(The voices break off as if cut with a knife.)

ROLAND. Shapes of dust and fancy! Unreal voices!
But where is the voice that launched me on my road?
Where is the shape the first that I remember?
Why doesn't *she* appear—even in fancy?
It is the least she could—Mother, where are you?
Yes, you; I'm calling you—my mother who sent me forth—
It was all your doing. But for you
I who had no beliefs of my own,
I who had no will of my own,
Should not be here today pursuing
A dark tower that is only dark
Because it does not exist. And Mother!
It is only your will that drives me still
As signified in the blood-red stone
I wear on my finger under my glove
That burns me like a living weal.

(suddenly puzzled)

. . . Burns me? . . . Burns me? . . . It always has—
But have I gone numb? I can feel nothing.
Off with this glove! I *can't* believe that—

(A chord from the orchestra.)

ROLAND. The ring! The ring!
The colour is gone; the blood has gone out of it.
But that must mean . . . that means . . . .

MOTHER'S VOICE *(in a different acoustic, whispering)*.

It means, my son, that I want you back.

ROLAND. And the Quest then?

MOTHER. Lapses.
On my deathbed I have changed my mind;
I am bearing now a child of stone.
He can go on the Quest. But you, Roland—come back!
(*A pause while Roland takes in the implications.*)

ROLAND. The ring . . . is always right.
Recall! Reprieve! A thousand years of sunshine!
And the apples will be in bloom round Sylvie's house.
Was that my mother's voice? Look at the ring.
It is as pale as death, there is no more breach of duty,
Her will is not behind me. Breach of duty?
If she is dying, *there* is the breach of duty—
Not to be there. Mother, you sent me out
And I went out. Now that you call me back
I will come back! The desert take this ring—
It serves no further purpose!
(*An orchestral clink as he throws away the ring.*)

ROLAND (*startled*).
What was that?
It must have struck something hard. That's the first
Sound I've heard in the desert. Where did I throw
that ring?
A stone? But a carved stone! Looks like a milestone.
As if the desert had any use for milestones!
(*with a hysterical half-laugh*)
How many miles to Babylon? Let's see now;
These letters are choked with sand, 'To Those . . .
To Those . . .'
(*He deciphers the inscription, reading it aloud slowly.*)
'To Those Who Did Not Go Back—
Whose Bones being Nowhere, their signature is for
All Men—
Who went to their Death of their Own Free Will
Bequeathing Free Will to Others.'

(The Bird Voices cut in, in a different acoustic, jeering.)

PARROT. Pretty Polly! A tall story!

RAVEN. Caw-caw! And not so new!

PARROT. Pretty Polly! Unknown warriors!

RAVEN. Caw-caw! Nobody cares!

PARROT. 'Who went to their death!'—Pretty Polly!

RAVEN. 'Of their own free will!'—Caw-caw!

ROLAND. Of their own free will? It wasn't like that with me.
It was my mother pushed me to this point
And now she pulls me back. Let's see this ring —
Where's it fallen? Hm. Yes, there's no mistake,
Red no longer: my mother wants me back
And indeed it is high time; this desert has no end
Nor even any contour, the blank horizon
Retreats and yet retreats; without either rise or fall
Repeats, retreats, defeats; there is no sign of a tower—
You could see a tower for miles; there is not even a knoll,
Flatness is all—and nothing. Own free will?

(He has been speaking quietly but now bursts out.)

As if I Roland had ever . . . . Tutors, trumpeters, women,
Old soaks and crooked stewards, everyone I have met
Has played his music on me. Own free will!
Three words not one of which I understand!
All right, Mother dear, I'm coming.

(Pause.)

Now . . . Where are my footsteps? Better follow them back.
Back to the forest and through it and so to the shore of the sea.
Are these my footsteps? But how small they look!
Well, you're a small man, Roland—Better admit it—

You'll be still smaller now . . . But are these my footsteps?
They are so near together—and I thought
I was walking with great strides! O Roland, Roland,
You thought yourself a hero—and you walked
With little steps like that! Now you must watch
These niggling foot-prints all your return journey
To underline your shame. What's shame to me
Who never had free will? . . . 'their own free will
Bequeathing free will to others.' Others indeed!
I begin to think my drunken friend was right
In his subjective tavern; there are no others
Apart from the projections of my mind
And, once that mind is empty, man's a desert.

(*losing his temper*)

Others! Who are these others? Where can I find 'em?

CHILD'S VOICE (*out of the blue*).

Nowhere, Roland. Nowhere.

ROLAND. There! What did I say? There *are* no—

CHILD'S VOICE.

You will never find us if you go forward—
For you will be dead before we are born.
You will never find us if you go back—
For you will have killed us in the womb.

ROLAND. What! So I'm an infanticide now?

CHILD'S VOICE.

Not yet. But if you go back . . .

ROLAND. Who said I was going back?

CHILD'S VOICE.

I thought you had made up your mind.

ROLAND. I never make up my mind!

Didn't I say that my mother—Look, I'll leave it to chance;
Chance is as good an arbiter as any.

Watch me, you unborn children. See this tiny cactus?
I will strip it leaf by leaf—let that decide—
This Year, Next Year, Eena-Meena—*you* know the game, you unborn children.
Now.

(He counts in regular time, but with growing tension, as he picks off the leaves.)

Forward—back; forward—back; forward—back—forward;
Back—forward; back—forward; back—forward—back;
Forward—back; forward—back; forward—back—forward;
Back—forward; back—forward; back—forward—BACK.
There! The voice of chance. The oracle of the cactus.
Back! Back! That's what the cactus says.
But *I'm* . . .

(He holds the suspense, then with decision.)

. . . going forward, children!
Did you think that I'd let a cactus dictate to me?
Mother, don't pull on the string; you must die alone.
Forgive me, dear, but—I tell you I'm going forward.
Forward, Roland . . . into the empty desert,
Where all is flat and colourless and silent.

(He pauses; the orchestra creeps in with a heart-beat rhythm.)

Silent? . . . Then what's this?
Something new! A *sound*! But a sound of what?
Don't say that it's my heart! Why, Roland you poor fool,
Who would think you had one? You must be afraid;
It is fear reveals the heart.

(Heart-beat louder.)

ROLAND. Aha, you piece of clockwork—

Trying to have your little say while you can!
Before your wheels run down here in the empty desert.
(Sudden chord; the heart-beat continues.)
Empty? . . . Where have those mountains come from?
Closing round in a ring. Hump-backed horrors
That want to be in at the death. And where's the horizon?
A moment ago this was level. What's the game?
A confidence trick? A trap! I am cooped in.
A circle of ugly cliffs—a lobster-pot of rock!
Silence, my stupid heart! This looks like . . . looks like what?
This looks like the great circus in Ancient Rome,
Only there is no audience—and no lions.

(suddenly noticing)

No audience?
(Chord; heart-beat behind—and steadily increasing.)
No audience! Why, that's Gavin on top of that peak!
And Michael and Denis and Henry and Roger and John!
And men that I've never seen—in outlandish clothes,
Some of them even in armour. And there's Blind Peter—
With sight in his eyes, for he's pointing—
And my father too—I remember him from the album—
And my tutor—he must be dead—looking graver than ever
And—well to the front of course—my dear old Sergeant-Trumpeter.

(Figure in the music; the succeeding voices, other than Roland's own, sound as if coming from somewhere far-off and above.)

SERGEANT-TRUMPETER.

Roland! Hold the note at the end.

GAVIN. Be ready, old boy. This is it!

BLIND PETER.
Strike a good blow to avenge Blind Peter.

FATHER. Your heritage, my son. You were born to fight and—

ROLAND. Fight? Fight whom? This circus has no lions.

TUTOR. No lions, Roland? Have you forgotten your lessons?
I never mentioned lions; it was a dragon—
And only that for lack of a better name.

ROLAND. Yes, yes, dragon of course—but you told me, my good tutor,
The Dragon would not appear until I came to the Tower
And until I had blown my blast—Well, there is no tower!

GAVIN. That fooled *me*, Roland my brother.

FATHER. Look over there, Roland my son.

ROLAND. Where? . . . Oh *that* little thing?
Like a wart coming out of the ground!

FATHER. It's growing, Roland, it's growing.

TUTOR. You should recognise it from my lectures.

BLIND PETER.
That's the joker all right.

(*Figure in the music.*)

GAVIN. The tower! The Dark Tower!

SERGEANT-TRUMPETER.
Quick now, my lad. Unsling your trumpet.

ROLAND. But—

FATHER. It's growing, my son; waste no time.

ROLAND. It's growing; yes, it's growing.

CHILD'S VOICE.
Growing! Ooh! Look at it.
Strike a good blow for us unborn children.

MOTHER (*closer than the rest*).
And strike a blow for all dead mothers.

GAVIN. Jump to it, Roland.

FATHER. Waste no time.

SERGEANT-TRUMPETER.
Remember that challenge call.
Blow it the way I taught you.

ROLAND (*beginning quiet but resolute and building*).
Yes, dear friends, I will blow it the way you taught me.
I Roland, the black sheep, the unbeliever—
Who never did anything of his own free will—
Will do this now to bequeath free will to others.
(*full out*) Ahoy there, tower, Dark Tower, you're getting big,
Your shadow is cold upon me. What of that?
And you, you Dragon or whatever you are
Who make men beasts, come out—here is a man;
Come out and do your worst.

(*The heart-beat, having reached its crescendo, ends clean.*)

ROLAND (*restrained, in the sudden silence*).
Wrist be steady
As I raise the trumpet so—now fill my lungs—

(*The Challenge Call rings out; the Sergeant-Trumpeter speaks as the last long note is reached.*)

SERGEANT-TRUMPETER.
Good lad, Roland. Hold that note at the end.

(*The trumpet holds it, enriched and endorsed by the orchestra. They come to a full close and that is* THE END.)

SUNBEAMS IN HIS HAT

a study of Tchehov

as a man

TO

LAURENCE GILLIAM

CAST

Sunbeams in his Hat was first broadcast[1] in the B.B.C. Home Service on July 16th, 1944. The main parts, in order of their appearance, were played as follows:

FRAU SCHMIDT	MARCELLA SALZER
OLGA KNIPPER	MARTITA HUNT
TCHEHOV	ALAN WHEATLEY
TCHEHOV'S FATHER	IVOR BARNARD
MASSEUR	RICHARD WILLIAMS★
GENERAL	CYRIL GARDINER★
NURSE	MOLLY RANKIN★
BOY IN SAHALIN	MALCOLM THOMAS
'DORN'	GERALD CASE★
TOLSTOY	ALEXANDER SARNER★
GORKI	DUNCAN MCINTYRE★
'ARTEM'	HARRY HUTCHISON★
NEMIROVICH-DANCHENKO	CHARLES MAUNSELL★
DR. SCHWÖRER	HOWARD MARION-CRAWFORD

Gregori Tcherniak played Russian folk tunes on the balalaika.

Production by the author.

[1] An earlier version entitled *Dr Chekhov* was produced by Stephen Potter for the B.B.C. on September 6th, 1941.

INTRODUCTORY NOTE

Sunbeams in his Hat is the only programme in this book which was properly a *feature*.[1] 'Feature', as distinct from 'play', is the B.B.C. name for a dramatised broadcast which is primarily either informative or propagandist (propaganda here being taken to include the emotive celebration of anniversaries and gestures of homage—or of hatred—to anyone or anything dead or alive). Features therefore, having an enormous diversity of subject, have also a great diversity of form. Some of them are as loosely constructed as scrap-books, others come near to the unities and emotional impact of a play. The script here published belongs to the comparatively clearcut type of feature-biography (or feature-historical-portrait). Tchehov was given to me as a subject for homage in 1941, and I rewrote the programme in 1944 for the anniversary of his death. It was assumed that, like all decent feature-biographers, I would give accurate information about him. My own special intention was to correct the popular fallacy which uses the word Tchehov as a synonym for melancholia and which, incidentally, vitiates so many English productions of his plays.

The basic problem of such a portrait is condensation[2]—how to select a few significant 'shots' and put them coherently together in a little space. For this programme I used the method of the *flash-back*. Beginning with Tchehov on the morning of the day of his death I ended with him that evening; phases of his earlier life were presented through flash-backs. This method can be confusing and irritating, though when it comes off it provides tension and unity. The flash-backs in *Sunbeams in his Hat* are not,

[1] The two March Hare programmes, being satirical topical fantasies (negative propaganda or un-homage), were also, I think correctly, classified as features—but they are far from being what the word evokes in the mind of a B.B.C. planner.

[2] In condensing here I fear I omitted much that was very important, e.g. Tchehov's early phase of hard and distasteful hack-work.

I think, confusing but I would not deny that they may irritate. If so, it is not so much the fault of the flash-back scenes themselves as of the lead-ins to them from the preceding scenes; it was in the character of both Tchehov and Olga Knipper to be reminiscent and exchange expressions of homesickness but such reminiscences, just because they come so pat, are only too likely to sound stoogey. Still they remain, I think, preferable to the cold-fish voice of the Narrator.

While in nearly all features some amount of invented detail is necessary—and transpositions in time and place are on occasion permitted—this Tchehov programme is based very closely on fact, even his terms of endearment having been cribbed from his letters. This amount of realism affected of course my writing of dialogue. In my Introduction to *Christopher Columbus* I wrote that 'the radio play (if not the radio feature) can only reach its heights when the subject is slightly larger, or at least simpler, than life and the treatment is to some extent 'stylised' '. I would now italicise that parenthesis and add that even with plays the remark may mislead (especially if 'heights' is taken as equivalent to excellence). Selection of material alone will obviously both simplify and to some extent 'stylise' but larger-than-lifeness need not be part of the recipe; in a programme called *He Had a Date* I attempted the chronicle of a fictitious young man of our time and characterised him throughout by understatement and, while I did not succeed with him, I see nothing wrong in the method (though I admit that *indiscriminate* understatement has ruined the modern theatre).

So with Tchehov, I never made him more articulate—or poetic—than he himself could have been. I aimed at a dialogue that should be easy but exact, that without appearing to press him should give away things to the listener. As to stylisation in the poetic sense, I did fall back at the end of the programme, where such effects seem more needed, on the device of a *dream* (though this dream itself was based on fact). For a dream, besides being of its nature foreboding, allows also the echoing—probably with a 'twist'—of voices heard before. This device, like the flash-back proper, can easily be abused. In another feature-portrait, of Lauro de Bosis, where the hero's whole last Act takes place in the solitude of an aeroplane, I used a similar trick at considerable length because so long a soliloquy was out of the question. But I had not this excuse with Tchehov. My real reason, I think, for introducing the dream of the River was to get a more supple transition, a better prelude to the death itself, than could have been contrived through any further dialogue between Tchehov and his wife—that is, if I kept her in character.

SUNBEAMS IN HIS HAT

(*We hear a band playing in Badenweiler—July 1904. The band ends as the voices begin.*)

FRAU SCHMIDT (*gushing*). Good morning, Madame Tchehov.

OLGA KNIPPER. Good morning, Frau Schmidt.

FRAU SCHMIDT. It's going to be hot again, I think.

OLGA KNIPPER. Hot, Frau Schmidt? Purgatory!

FRAU SCHMIDT. You don't like the heat?

OLGA KNIPPER. Me, Frau Schmidt? Oh, *I* don't mind the heat. It's my husband.

FRAU SCHMIDT. I beg your pardon, how stupid I am. How is your dear husband today?

OLGA KNIPPER. Oh, a bit better, a little bit better, but you know, my dear—well, the last three days have been terrible. Dr. Schwörer came in two days ago and told me I must be prepared . . . .

FRAU SCHMIDT. Prepared . . . for what?

OLGA KNIPPER (*changing the subject*). Exquisite!

FRAU SCHMIDT. What?

OLGA KNIPPER. That shaft of sunlight away over there on the forest. In half an hour or so we'll have sun here on the verandah.

FRAU SCHMIDT. But, Madame Tchehov, you were saying . . . about Dr. Schwörer— ?

OLGA KNIPPER. Oh, Dr. Schwörer? A charming man, and he knows when to put his foot down. Anton, you know, wants to pack up his bags. He wants to get out of here at once.

FRAU SCHMIDT. But you have not been long in Badenweiler.

OLGA KNIPPER. My dear Frau Schmidt, we've been three weeks here—and Anton thinks it's eternity.

FRAU SCHMIDT. Your husband doesn't *like* Badenweiler?

OLGA KNIPPER. He's panting to go to Italy. Lake Como, you know. Or, better still, home to Russia.

FRAU SCHMIDT. Geniuses of course are so restless. I always tell my daughter she must never marry a writer.

(*Tinkle of doorbell.*)

OLGA KNIPPER. Quite right, Frau Schmidt. Never marry a writer—especially when he's a genius. There's Anton now.

(*Tinkle of doorbell.*)

The masseur comes to see him at seven-thirty and Anton likes to talk to me first.

FRAU SCHMIDT. Well, remember me to him, Madame Tchehov, and I hope . . . I hope all will be well. If you were to lose him . . . the loss . . . well, the loss, Madame Tchehov, would be a loss to humanity.

(*Tinkle of bell.*)

OLGA KNIPPER. Thank you, Frau Schmidt. I must run.

FRAU SCHMIDT. Goodbye, Madame Tchehov.

OLGA KNIPPER. Goodbye, Frau Schmidt.

FRAU SCHMIDT. Goodbye, Madame Tchehov.

(*The German band begins again—and continues.*)

OLGA. Anton?

TCHEHOV. Ah, there you are, Olga, my poppet. Where have you been?

OLGA. Talking to Frau Schmidt. She wants to be remembered to you.

TCHEHOV. Frau Schmidt? Frau Schmidt? Oh, the woman who's all over braid.

OLGA. Yes. Face like a pudding.

TCHEHOV. Why *do* they dress so badly? German taste, if there *is* such a thing—(*Fit of coughing*)

OLGA. There, Antosha, there!

(*The band continues while he gets over his coughing.*)

TCHEHOV. What were we saying? Oh, yes, German taste . . . What do they pay that band?

OLGA. How should *I* know, dear? More than they ever pay *us* at the Moscow Art—

TCHEHOV (*interrupting her, with a sudden change of tone*). The Moscow Art theatre . . . Pigeon, we must go back to Russia!

OLGA. Later, Antosha, later.

TCHEHOV. No, Olga. At once! First we'll go to Trieste and then a steamer for Odessa and then—

OLGA. Dr. Schwörer says—

TCHEHOV. I don't give a damn what Dr. Schwörer says. These German doctors have stood me on my head. Doctors? I'm one myself. What's the date, my goldfish?

OLGA. Second of July.

TCHEHOV. July already? High time I was cured. (*facetiously*) In fact, now I think of it . . . I *am* cured.

OLGA. Now, Antosha, Dr. Schwörer—

TCHEHOV. Dr. Schwörer can drown himself in the Rhine! Doctor Tchehov says Anton Tchehov is cured. But he won't stay cured much longer if he has to listen to this band—seven o'clock every morning, seven o'clock every evening . . . .

(*The band comes into the foreground.*)

OLGA. Shall I close the windows?

TCHEHOV. No, no, don't close the windows. I must have air.

(*Short fit of coughing; during the following speeches the band fades away.*)

TCHEHOV. I wish I could do with this band what one does with the rhythm of a train. You know, poppet, how one sits in a train and the train goes chuggity-chug, chuggity-chug, chuggity-chug, with infinite monotony, but as you listen, you can change it into any rhythm you like—the poems of Pushkin or . . . or . . .

OLGA. Or the Serenade for Strings by Tchaikovsky—

TCHEHOV. Yes, or the hymns in church when I was a little boy and father made us sing in the choir.
In Taganrog, that was.

(*coughing*)

I don't like churches but I *did* like those hymns.

(*His voice grows distant.*)

The ikons were pretty too. Father was determined we should all grow up Christians—

(*Out of the distance comes an Orthodox Greek Church Choir.*)

TCHEHOV'S FATHER (*roughish voice*). Anton, you must believe in God.

CHILD'S VOICE. Yes, father.

FATHER. Alexander, Nikolay, Anton, Ivan—You must all believe in God.

CHILD'S VOICE. Yes, father.

(*The choir in the background stops singing.*)

FATHER. Put your trust in God and everything will go well. Think of what Grandfather did.

CHILD'S VOICE. What did Grandfather do?

FATHER. You know that your grandfather used to be a serf. In the bad old days before serfdom was abolished. To be a serf—that was a terrible thing, but your grandfather trusted in God. He saved up his money, penny by penny, until he had saved—how much? How much do you think?

CHILD'S VOICE. How much?

FATHER. Three thousand five hundred roubles.

CHILD'S VOICE. My!

FATHER. He bought his family freedom at seven hundred roubles per head. The good God smiled on his labours. Are you listening, Anton?

CHILD'S VOICE. Yes, father.

FATHER. Fear God and you cannot go wrong. You see this shop of mine—'Colonial Produce: P. E. Tchehov'? I didn't always have this shop—

CHILD'S VOICE. Didn't you?

FATHER. No, my children. For a long, long time I worked as a clerk; the hours were long and hard and the money was very little. But I trusted in God and I put my pennies in a box. So at last the day came, I stopped being a clerk, I bought a business of my own. I bought this business and God made it prosper—'Colonial Produce: P. E. Tchehov'. So you see, my children: fear God and you cannot go wrong. Alexander, Nikolay, Anton, Ivan, fear God and you cannot go wrong . . . .

(His voice thins outwards like a ripple, overlaps back into the present.)

TCHEHOV. 'Fear God and you cannot go wrong . . .'. When I was in my 'teens my father's shop went bankrupt. He had to move to Moscow. In Moscow he again became a clerk. They paid him a starvation wage.

(Knocking on the door—but he disregards it. He has probably told her all this before, but is reminiscing for his own sake.)

TCHEHOV. The rest of the family went to Moscow too; they all starved together. That's why my brother Nikolay later became consumptive. Moscow was the beginning—

(Repeated knocking.)

OLGA. That will be the masseur. Herein! Herein!

(Pause.)

OLGA. Good morning, Monsieur Legrand.

MASSEUR. Good morning, Madame. Good morning, Monsieur. And how are we today?

TCHEHOV (*switching at once to his 'funny' manner*). We have just found out we are cured. We are chock full of butter and porridge. That is one thing these Germans can do—they make the most beautiful porridge.

MASSEUR. Monsieur has such a sense of humour . . . . Well, we had better start work. First, please, will you lie on your front? So. Now please, Madame, where is the basin of water?

TCHEHOV. Having massage is really a treat. It makes me think of my mongoose.

MASSEUR. Of your *what*?

TCHEHOV. He liked being stroked so much.

MASSEUR. Who did, Monsieur?

OLGA. His mongoose, Monsieur Legrand.

TCHEHOV. I brought him back from Sahalin.

MASSEUR. From where, Monsieur?

OLGA. Please, Monsieur Legrand, don't ask so many questions.

TCHEHOV. From Sahalin. Otherwise called Hell. (*He groans.*)

MASSEUR. Am I hurting you? Then turn a little more on your side . . . . That's right.

TCHEHOV. If you ever want to go to Hell . . . .

MASSEUR. Monsieur has such a sense of—

TCHEHOV (*suddenly serious again, though 'throwing it away'*). A sense of reality, my friend. Sahalin is one of our penal settlements. If you want to see humanity at its worst—

MASSEUR. But I do *not*, Monsieur.

TCHEHOV. You are mistaken then. If you like humanity you have to see the dregs of it. You know where Sahalin is? An island south of Kamchatka and north of Japan. The dreariest, dirtiest outpost of Holy Russia. To get there—

MASSEUR. A moment, Monsieur. Still more over on your side . . . . Good.

TCHEHOV. First you take a steamer down the Volga, then you take a steamer up the Kama. A river that looks like coffee slops. Then you tackle Siberia . . . .

OLGA. I can never think, Anton, why you went there.

TCHEHOV. Nobody could. They all thought I was mad.

MASSEUR. I imagine, Madame, your husband was looking for copy.

TCHEHOV (*bursting out*). Copy! Copy! . . .

MASSEUR. Be careful, Monsieur, you will hurt yourself.

TCHEHOV. What do you mean by talking to me about copy?

MASSEUR. But surely, Monsieur, as a writer—

TCHEHOV. A writer! Don't you know I'm a doctor?

MASSEUR. Yes, of course, but—

TCHEHOV (*bitterly*). Well, forget I'm a writer. That's why I went to Sahalin. To get away from the people who called me a writer. I got the Pushkin Prize, so they thought they must ask me to dinner. And while I was eating their dinners my brother died of consumption. So I went to Sahalin. That was in 1890.

(*A steamer is heard hooting in the distance. The next speech, delivered quietly and rhythmically, is really a soliloquy.*)

TCHEHOV (*dreamily*). Down the Volga and up the Kama. Days of rain and days of snow. First there was mud and then there was snow and then there was dust. First there was killing cold and then there was killing heat . . . . Innumerable muddy rivers . . . . Endless plains where the wind sings in the stunted birch trees. Further and further from civilisation. Miles and miles of snow and desert—Russian snow and Russian desert. Russia? Poverty . . . distance . . . disease. Tomsk and Irkutsk . . . further and further.

(*Siberian music creeps in.*)

TCHEHOV. Further and further on the road to Sahalin. Further and further on the road to Hell.

(*The music swells up to place Tchehov in the past—and in Sahalin.*)

GENERAL (*a hearty type of Philistine*). Now that you're here, Anton Pavlovitch, what can we do for you? Why you've come here I can't for the life of me imagine, but—

TCHEHOV. I've come here to study the convicts.

GENERAL. God bless me, what an idea! Well, if you *really* want to study the convicts, just tell me what you require and I'll give you every facility. Now if you'd like to see a flogging—

TCHEHOV. Thank you, General. My idea is to make a kind of census.

GENERAL. A kind of what?

TCHEHOV. A census. I want to make a census of the whole population of Sahalin.

GENERAL. My very dear doctor! Do you know that the convicts alone run into thousands and thousands?

TCHEHOV. So much the better. My object—

GENERAL. I suppose you want to write a novel or something?

TCHEHOV. A novel, General? What do you think I am? I want to contribute something to medical science.

GENERAL. Very well, Doctor, it strikes me as rather eccentric, but I'll see what I can do for you. I'll give you a competent nurse to show you around the settlement.

(*Music to register an interval.*)

TCHEHOV. Who lives in there, nurse?

NURSE (*brutalised*). Don't know his name but the place is filthy.

(*Tchehov knocks on the door of a hovel.*)

NURSE. Don't go in there. You'll catch something.

TCHEHOV. I tell you I'm making a census.

NURSE. Digging your grave, you mean.

(*He knocks again.*)

NURSE. Leave this lot out. They're scum.

TCHEHOV (*quietly*). Scum? So are we all.

(*He knocks again.*)

NURSE. Thank goodness for that. No one at home.

TCHEHOV. Well, I'll just peep inside.

NURSE (*muttering*). Crazy! Plumb crazy . . . .

(*Pause while Tchehov enters the hovel. Inside his voice sounds different.*)

TCHEHOV. Terribly dark in here. Anyone in?

NURSE. Ach, the stink, the stink!

TCHEHOV. Anyone here? Anyone at home?

(*He is answered, as if from a corner, by a little boy's voice, very hostile.*)

BOY. *I'm* here.

TCHEHOV. Who are you, sonny? Come over here and talk to me.

BOY. Get out of my house.

TCHEHOV. Now, now . . . I'm not going to hurt you . . . . Have a sugar-stick.

NURSE. Doctor, I'll wait for you outside.

TCHEHOV. Nice, isn't it? . . . Now, sonny, what's your name?

BOY (*chewing*). Alyoshka . . . . What's yours?

TCHEHOV. Anton Pavlovitch . . . . How old are you?

BOY (*still not 'giving' anything*). Ten. How old are *you*?

TCHEHOV. Thirty. Isn't it old? (*Pause*) Do you live here with your father?

BOY. Yes.

TCHEHOV. What's your father's surname?

BOY. Don't know.

TCHEHOV. Don't know? You live with your father and you don't know his name!

BOY (*'dead-pan'*). He *isn't* my father.

TCHEHOV. But you said . . . . Now look here, Alyoshka, is he your father or isn't he?

BOY. Oh, *he* just lives with mother.

TCHEHOV. Your mother? Is she married or a widow?

BOY. Widow. Came down here with her husband.

TCHEHOV. Then what became of her husband?

BOY (*'dead-pan'*). Mother killed him.

TCHEHOV. What did you say?

BOY. Mother got tired. She killed him.

(*The Siberian music creeps in again. Tchehov makes a last effort.*)

TCHEHOV. Do you remember your father? Your real father?

BOY. Give me another sugar-stick.

TCHEHOV. But please tell me, Alyoshka—

BOY. Give me another sugar-stick.

(*The music comes up by itself to round off that fiasco, then gives place to the German band—and to Badenweiler.*)

TCHEHOV. So you *see*, Monsieur Legrand . . . ? That was a long time ago—fourteen years—but they still send convicts to Siberia, they still send convicts to Sahalin. Millions of lost souls, millions of broken bodies . . . I brought back a lot of statistics. Also a mongoose.

MASSEUR. And what did you do with your statistics?

TCHEHOV. Handed them over to our rotten bureaucracy. Tell me, Monsieur Legrand, you do not know our Russia?

MASSEUR. No, Monsieur, I have not that privilege, alas.

TCHEHOV. Then let me tell you. Russia is a huge . . . beautiful

. . . *monster*. A monster sunk in lethargy . . . destroying its children . . . destroying itself. Some day perhaps it will wake—

OLGA. Now, Antosha, don't go talking like Gorki . . . Monsieur Legrand will think you are dying of social consciousness.

TCHEHOV (*dryly*). I'm dying anyway, Olga.

(*An embarrassed pause while he picks up the thread he has broken; beginning again with precise emphasis.*)

TCHEHOV. There is one thing that's the ruin of Russia—

(*A short fit of coughing interrupts him.*)

MASSEUR. What is that, Monsieur?

TCHEHOV. *Ignorance*. Gross abysmal ignorance. The mother of all evils . . . from the Baltic to Vladivostock . . . Sahalin was a bottomless pit of ignorance. When I got back to Moscow—

MASSEUR (*still suave*). A happy day, I take it?

TCHEHOV. I found it was worse than Sahalin. All the nonsense began all over again. Literary salons . . . dinner parties . . . .

OLGA (*with forced cheerfulness, hoping to stop him moralising*). So you know what he did? He got together with his old friend Souvorin—

TCHEHOV. And we went to Monte Carlo.

MASSEUR. But why?

OLGA. They went to Monte Carlo and played roulette. They came back bankrupt.

MASSEUR. But I would not have thought . . . .

OLGA (*at last losing her patience*). You would not have thought what?

MASSEUR. Excuse me, but I do not understand. If Monsieur was worried with social problems—

OLGA. You wouldn't have thought he would flit to Monte Carlo. Well, he *did*. It seems quite natural to me.

MASSEUR. Natural, yes, but *logical* . . . ?

OLGA. Logic! A man goes round making censuses—writing reports about cholera—collecting subscriptions for hospitals

—in his off moments he writes short stories and plays—he becomes a master of literature—social conditions give him a nightmare—he shakes off the dust of Moscow—he takes the boat for Monte Carlo. You, Monsieur, are a Frenchman. You think this is all illogical. You think, if a man is appalled by his country's poverty, it's silly to go and play roulette—

TCHEHOV. It was silly, but it did me a world of good . . . . It cleaned out my pockets and it cleaned out my soul. Life recovered its tang. Souvorin—

OLGA. Poor old Souvorin! You led him a dance.

TCHEHOV (*gaily, almost boyishly*). He didn't need leading. How well I remember him standing there over the tables . . . . You know Monsieur Legrand, the Casino is marvellous. A really exquisite vulgarity—gilt and plush—crowds of bourgeois faces, all of them eau-de-nil in the light reflected from the tables. Even Souvorin had a green face. How well I remember it all. Just as if it were yesterday . . . yesterday . . . yesterday . . . .

(*A slight discreet babble drowns his reminiscing voice and brings to life his reminiscence.*)

CROUPIER. Faites vos jeux, messieurs et mesdames.

ENGLISHWOMAN. But can't you see, George—

TCHEHOV. Souvorin, watch the angry Englishwoman.

CROUPIER. Faites vos jeux, messieurs et mesdames.

ENGLISHWOMAN. Can't you *see*, George? You must let me put a louis on a *number*. What's the good of betting on a red. I *knew* 27 would turn up . . . .

HUSBAND. Emily, you make me sick. I didn't want to bring you here at all—

CROUPIER. Faites vox jeux, messieurs et mesdames.

ENGLISHWOMAN. I'm going to put this—all of it—on Number . . . Number . . . Number Eighteen.

HUSBAND. You're going to do nothing of the sort. You'll put it on Impair. An even chance, Emily, an even chance . . . .

(The camera, as it were, pans round the Casino; different voices emerge and disappear.)

VOICES. Numéro cinq . . . Rouge . . . Impair . . . Numéro Quatorze . . . Noir . . . etc.

SOUVORIN. Well, Antosha, had enough?

TCHEHOV (*in high spirits*). Enough? Certainly not. Look how angry the Englishwoman is; her husband won't let her bet on a number. What was the number she wanted?

SOUVORIN. Eighteen.

TCHEHOV. Right.

(We hear the clicking of the ball.)

CROUPIER. *Dix-huit.*

ENGLISHWOMAN (*furious*). George!

TCHEHOV. You see. She picked a winner.

SOUVORIN. But not for herself, poor thing.

ENGLISHWOMAN. George, those Russians! They betted on eighteen.

TCHEHOV. Souvorin, old man, my pockets are bulging.

SOUVORIN. Looks as if this is our day.

TCHEHOV (*lightly*). Boring if we win too much.

(From this point the scene is highly stylised; excited music begins here, faint at first but ever increasing in volume, while the dialogue gets faster and faster.)

1ST CROUPIER. Faites vos jeux, messieurs et mesdames.

2ND CROUPIER. Les jeux sont faits.

TCHEHOV. Two gold pieces on Number Seven.

2ND CROUPIER. Cinq.

1ST CROUPIER. Faites vos jeux, messieurs et mesdames.

TCHEHOV. On 19.

2ND CROUPIER. Quatorze.

SOUVORIN. There go another ten louis.

1ST CROUPIER. Les jeux sont faits.

2ND CROUPIER. Faites vos jeux.

TCHEHOV. Nine.

1ST CROUPIER. Vingt-et-un.

TCHEHOV. Twenty-three.

2ND CROUPIER. Cinq.

TCHEHOV. Five again. All right—cinq.

1ST CROUPIER. Les jeux sont faits.

2ND CROUPIER. Zéro.

TCHEHOV. Nineteen.

1ST CROUPIER. Quinze.

2ND CROUPIER. Faites vos jeux.

TCHEHOV. Seven.

1ST CROUPIER. Vingt-cinq.

2ND CROUPIER. Rien ne va plus.

TCHEHOV. Damn it. Impair.

1ST CROUPIER. Huit: Rouge: Pair.

2ND CROUPIER. Rien ne va plus.

TCHEHOV. Very well. Rouge.

1ST CROUPIER. Noir.

2ND CROUPIER. Rien ne va plus.

TCHEHOV. Noir.

1ST CROUPIER. Rouge.

2ND CROUPIER. Rien ne va plus.

TCHEHOV. Twenty.

1ST CROUPIER. Onze.

2ND CROUPIER. Rien ne va plus.

TCHEHOV. Seven.

1ST CROUPIER. Cinq.

2ND CROUPIER. Rien ne va plus.

(*The music here reaches its peak, then cuts out abruptly; a pause before Souvorin speaks in a dead silence.*)

SOUVORIN. What have you left, Antosha?

TCHEHOV (*with a laugh in his voice*). My return ticket to Nice.

BOTH CROUPIERS (*together and with unrealistic emphasis*). Rien ne va plus.

(*A pause—enough to return us to the present.*)

TCHEHOV. The band seems to have stopped, Olga.

OLGA. No more brass till seven this evening.

TCHEHOV. Thank God for that.

OLGA. Time for you to get up, Antosha. How do you feel now?

TCHEHOV. My massage did me good but Heavens . . . !

OLGA. Heavens what?

TCHEHOV. If I stay any longer among all this German peace and order!

OLGA. Longing for Russia?

TCHEHOV. Yes, and *you*? Longing for the Moscow Art Theatre?

OLGA. A little, Antosha, just a little.

TCHEHOV. Stanislavsky and Nemirovich-Danchenko and Artem and—

OLGA. Don't make me homesick.

TCHEHOV. You love the stage, don't you, my little beetle?

OLGA. Of course I do. It's my life.

TCHEHOV. A frightening invention . . . the stage. I never meant to get mixed up in it. No sensible man would be a playwright.

OLGA. How nice that you're not sensible!

TCHEHOV. The degradation, the prostitution, the fret and the flutter, the frightful disappointments—

OLGA. Disappointments?

TCHEHOV. Remember 'The Seagull'?

OLGA. Oh, the production in St. Petersburg? Once Stanislavsky produced it—

TCHEHOV. And you were its leading lady—well, that of course was different. But when they did it in St. Petersburg . . . and the bath-chair broke on the stage . . . .

(His voice gives place to the catcalls and laughs of a crowd. A hubbub continues through the following conversation in the wings.)

STAGE MANAGER. There goes the bath-chair, Anton Pavlovitch.

TCHEHOV. Never again! Never again!

STAGE MANAGER. Never again what?

TCHEHOV. You are a Stage Manager. Never again will I write for your medium.

STAGE MANAGER. You won't, eh? Well, Anton Pavlovitch, judging by the reactions of the house—

(A fresh outburst from the audience interrupts him.)

STAGE MANAGER. Judging, I said, by the reactions of the populace, I think your decision is correct. You *can't* write for the stage.

(The hubbub recedes, vanishes into the past.)

OLGA (*teasingly*). Never again, eh?

TCHEHOV. I meant it, too. If it hadn't been for Nemirovich-Danchenko—and Stanislavsky—and the whole Moscow Art—

OLGA. *We* did the 'Seagull' rather better. Didn't we, Anton darling? But, Lord, wasn't I frightened? And as for Stanislavsky . . . !

TCHEHOV. He felt that his life depended on it.

OLGA. *Your* life, Antosha, *your* life. It was just after all those haemorrhages. We were scared right to the end. To the scene where they bring in the beer and I'm centre stage behind the table and Trigorin's looking at that awful stuffed gull and then there's the shot in the wings and—

(She is cut off by a loud pistol shot. After a pause she speaks again, now 'throwing her voice' as on the stage.)

OLGA (*as Madame Arkadin*). What's that?

'DORN'. That's nothing. Must be something gone off in my medicine-chest. Don't be anxious . . . .

(A door opens—and after a pause, closes.)

'DORN'. That's what it is. A bottle of ether exploded.

(He begins to hum.)

OLGA (*as Madam Arkadin*). 'Ough, how frightened I was . . . . It reminded me of how . . . . It made me quite dizzy.

'DORN'. Seen this magazine, Trigorin? There's an article here . . . from America . . . I wanted to ask you, among other things . . . as I'm very much interested in the question . . . .

(*intimate*) Get Irina Nikolayevna away somehow. The fact is, Konstantin Gavrilitch has shot himself.'

(*A slight pause—and applause breaks out from the audience; then fades away slowly, bringing Olga back to the present.*)

OLGA. Yes, indeed, we did it a great deal better. And then Uncle Vanya. Remember that speech of mine in the second Act? When my husband's gone off to have his lime-flower tea and Vanya is complaining that he's had no sleep and I just despair about the whole household. 'It's dreadful—' how does it begin—'It's dreadful . . .'?

TCHEHOV (*feeling for the lines*). 'It's dreadful in this house. Your mother hates everything except her pamphlets and the Professor—'

OLGA (*as Yelena*). 'The Professor is irritated, he does not trust me, and is afraid of you; Sonya is angry with her father, angry with me and hasn't spoken to me for a fortnight; you hate my husband and show open contempt for your mother; I am overwrought and have been nearly crying twenty times today . . . . It's dreadful in this house . . .'.

TOLSTOY (*on echo, with angry emphasis*). It certainly is but what *is* the point of writing like this? What is the point, what is the point . . .?

OLGA. Everyone loved it. And the flowers I got!

TCHEHOV. Tolstoy didn't love it.

OLGA. Oh well, Tolstoy! Just shook his head and—

TOLSTOY (*on echo*). 'What is the point? What is the point?'

TCHEHOV. Tolstoy wanted a moral.

OLGA. He would. Dreary old thing!

TCHEHOV. No, no, my poppet. Not dreary.

OLGA. Well, look at Gorki. Gorki—

TCHEHOV. Gorki has a different view of art.

OLGA. He certainly has. Remember that row in Yalta? We were all sitting out on the terrace and someone was playing a guitar behind the big eucalyptus tree—

TCHEHOV. Yalta? Yes. That wasn't life, that was raspberries and cream.

OLGA. The cream had turned a bit *that* day. If it hadn't been for the guitar . . . going on in spite of those two . . . .

(*A guitar steals in, adjusting the focus to Yalta.*)

TOLSTOY. Gorki, you're utterly wrong . . . . What do *you* think, Anton Pavlovitch?

TCHEHOV (*humorously deprecating*). Me? I don't know about Art. I don't know what the word means.

GORKI. Well, you can't agree with Tolstoy!

TOLSTOY. Anton Pavlovitch, don't be so feeble. You *must* have views on the subject. The problem of Art—

TCHEHOV. *Is* there a 'problem of Art'? A writer—

GORKI. A writer must be true to his inspiration.

TCHEHOV. Nonsense, Maxim. A writer should have eyes in his head and a knowledge of life. A writer is just like a chemist, he's got to be objective. As objective as a chemist—

TOLSTOY. The writer's function is to better the world.

GORKI. Better it in what way? Encourage people to lie down under oppression? Encourage the masses to starve and—

TOLSTOY. Encourage people to put their hopes upon God.

GORKI. And by that you mean give up their hopes of humanity.

TOLSTOY (*Thumping on the table*). Humanity! Maxim Gorki, you are nothing but a . . . a sentimental would-be revolutionary.

GORKI. Sentimental! What do you call yourself? *You*, Leo Nikolaevitch Tolstoy—a white-gloved landlord posing as a peasant.

TOLSTOY. And you are just a young peasant who can't digest his ideas.

GORKI. There is only *one* idea—

TOLSTOY. One idea is more than *you* can manage, Maxim. When you are ten years older—

GORKI. Perhaps I will give up trying? You want me to give up trying. You want—

TOLSTOY. What do *you* think, Anton Pavlovitch?

GORKI. Yes, what do *you* think?

OLGA. Anton doesn't think anything. He's busy.

TOLSTOY. Anton Pavlovitch! What on earth are you doing with your hat?

(*The guitar begins again.*)

TCHEHOV (*would-be naïve*). I'm trying to catch a sunbeam.

GORKI. What?

TCHEHOV. If I can catch a sunbeam, catch it in my hat, then I can put it on my head and . . . .

(*They drown him in peals of laughter—their argument forgotten. As the laughter thins out, the guitar shows through it. Then Tolstoy speaks, half choking.*)

TOLSTOY. Anton Pavlovitch, you are incorrigible.

(*They all laugh again—with and at Tolstoy. The guitar takes over the foreground, then breaks off.*)

OLGA. Lord, how I laughed. And Tolstoy—I thought his beard would come off. That was the way to deal with him. Sunbeams . . . sunbeams in your hat!

TCHEHOV (*quietly*). Maybe he was right all the same.

OLGA. Who was right? Tolstoy?

TCHEHOV. Yes. Or maybe Gorki.

OLGA. They can't both have been right.

TCHEHOV. They can both have been right in contrast to me. The artist must grind an axe: Tolstoy thinks so, Gorki thinks so —of course they are different axes. But poor Anton Pavlovitch—he just hasn't got an axe to grind. Even Souvorin used to rebuke me for it. He said I was indifferent to good and evil.

OLGA. What nonsense, Antosha.

TCHEHOV. Gorki, now—he thinks that Art is the handmaid of Progress. And progress of course means Revolution. According to Gorki, the writer must have a political platform. Politics—

OLGA. Damn his politics. If Gorki wants to go in for propaganda, he's welcome. You and I, Antosha, we know what Art really means.

TCHEHOV. Oh no, we don't.

OLGA. Nonsense, Antosha. These people like Gorki who want you to write propaganda—they don't understand that you're not a political hack. You're first and foremost a playwright.

TCHEHOV. I am first and foremost an ordinary person. Secondly I'm a doctor. Thirdly I'm a writer of short stories—but not so good as Maupassant. Fourth—and a very poor fourth it is —I am a writer of Vaudeville.

OLGA. Antosha, you're maddening. Vaudeville indeed! When the crowning point of your career was . . . .

TCHEHOV (*coldly*). Was what?

OLGA. The first performance of 'The Cherry Orchard'.

TCHEHOV. Oh, *that*? That's Ancient History anyway.

OLGA. Ancient History? January of this year!

TCHEHOV (*genuinely forgetful*). Was it?

OLGA. Your Jubilee, my sweet!

TCHEHOV. Oh yes, yes, my Jubilee. As if I was a politician or a Grand Duke or a sanitary inspector or someone. If only I could have got out of going to the theatre!

OLGA. And missed your wife as Madame Ranevsky?

TCHEHOV (*slowly with feeling*). No . . . I wouldn't have missed that!

(*An actress is heard playing her part in the distance. Her voice comes nearer and nearer. It is Olga.*)

OLGA (*as Madame Ranevsky*). 'Oh, my childhood, my innocence! It was in this nursery I used to sleep, from here I looked out into the orchard, happiness waked with me every morning, and in those days the orchard was just the same, nothing has changed. (*Laughs with delight.*) All, all white! Oh, my orchard! After the dark, gloomy autumn and the cold winter; you are young again and full of happiness, the heavenly angels have never left you . . . . If I could cast off the burden that weighs on my heart, if I could forget the past!'

(Pause)

TCHEHOV. No, my goldfish, I wouldn't have missed that.

OLGA. 'If I could forget the past . . .'. When you wrote those lines, Anton, how far . . . how far was that yourself?

TCHEHOV. Myself? Not at all, silly. *I'm* not a Tchehov character. Except, in so far as the Cherry Orchard's concerned . . . .

OLGA. Except what?

TCHEHOV. Well, the curtain, you know. Everyone must have a curtain. In a cherry orchard or . . . Badenweiler. Old age in one case, T.B. in another. Artem was good in that last speech.

OLGA. Yes, wasn't he good? I watched him from the wings. Shambling in in those slippers—I wonder they didn't come off—and trying the handles of the doors and then coming forwards towards the audience.

ARTEM (*as Firs*). 'They have gone. . . . They have forgotten me. . . . . Never mind . . . I'll sit here a bit. . . . I'll be bound Leonid Andreyevitch hasn't put his fur coat on and has gone off in his thin overcoat. (*Sighs anxiously.*) I didn't see after him. These young people . . . (*mutters unintelligibly*). Life has slipped by as though I hadn't lived. . . . I'll lie down a bit. . . . There's no strength in you, nothing left at all. Oh, you good-for-nothing!

(Stage sound as of breaking harp-strings: silence: ovation.)

STANISLAVSKY (*from stage*). Ladies and gentlemen,

(Cheering)

Ladies and gentlemen, will you please remain in your seats.

MALE VOICE. That's Stanislavsky.

FEMALE VOICE. Who's that in the middle?

MALE VOICE. The other director—Nemirovich-Danchenko. The empty chair is for the author.

FEMALE VOICE. Where *is* the author?

VOICES. Author! Author! Where is Anton Pavlovitch?

MALE VOICE. There he comes—

(Terrific cheering.)

FEMALE VOICE. Doesn't he look ill? Quite transparent! And what a shabby grey suit! Of course they say that it's both lungs now. I'd have thought all the same . . . .

MALE VOICE. Hush! Danchenko's going to make a speech.

DANCHENKO. Ladies and gentlemen—

(Clapping and cheering.)

DANCHENKO (*rather pompously*). Ladies and gentlemen, on behalf of the Moscow Art Theatre and my co-director, Konstantin Sergeievitch Stanislavsky—

(Still louder clapping and cheering.)

DANCHENKO (*emotionally*). I wish to thank you all. . . . I have not words to express it. . . . I wish to thank you all for your wonderful reception of this play.

Secondly . . . on behalf of the whole company . . . and also of you, the audience, I wish to say a few words in homage to the author of this play, Anton Pavlovitch Tchehov—

(Enormous cheering.)

DANCHENKO. This, my friends, is a special occasion. It is Anton Pavlovitch's birthday. It is also the Jubilee of his literary career. Anton Pavlovitch, I address you on behalf of the Moscow Art Theatre. Without you our theatre would be nowhere. The debt that we owe you is beyond all words. Your heaven-sent talent, your generous heart, your *soul*. . . . My friends, the Moscow Art Theatre is *Tchehov's* theatre, Tchehov is the main-spring of our art. Tchehov is the sun that has ripened our endeavours. Tchehov is—

(Wild cheering.)

DANCHENKO. Anton Pavlovitch, I wish to ask you . . . perhaps you will speak to us yourself?

(Pause.)

OLGA (*in low voice*). He *won't* speak. He's exhausted.

STANISLAVSKY (*in low voice*). He can't speak. He mustn't.

DANCHENKO. Will you do us the great honour, Anton Pavlovitch—?

STANISLAVSKY (*aside to Olga*). Why can't they leave him alone?

OLGA. Danchenko mustn't make him speak.

(*Pause.*)

DANCHENKO. My friends, Anton Pavlovitch regrets that he cannot address you himself—he is feeling too tired—but he thanks you all from his heart—

VOICE FROM AUDIENCE. *We* thank *him*!

DANCHENKO. Anton Pavlovitch thanks you all for everything and now that he is saying goodbye—

VOICE FROM AUDIENCE. Goodbye? Why goodbye?

DANCHENKO. Anton Pavlovitch is going abroad for his health. He is going to spend some time in—(*he feels for the name*) Badenweiler.

(*Slight pause; then the German band, fading up, materialises Badenweiler.*)

OLGA. It must be seven o'clock, Dr. Schwörer. There's that band.

DR. SCHWÖRER. Seven o'clock, Madame Tchehov? Time for your husband's supper. . . . Seven o'clock indeed! I must be toddling home.

OLGA. And you really think Anton is better?

DR. SCHWÖRER. Better, Madame? You must understand me. When I say 'better', the term is merely relative. His condition yesterday made me very anxious. Today—

OLGA. Today he's as gay as a schoolboy. He's been telling stories and roaring with laughter. If only he could get a proper sleep—

DR. SCHWÖRER. Well, remember what I told you. Before he goes to bed, a cup of strawberry tea.

OLGA. I give him it, Herr Doktor, but it doesn't seem to help much . . . and he's kept awake by the clock in his bedroom.

DR. SCHWÖRER. Clock? Take the clock away.

OLGA. It's a grandfather clock, a fixture . . . and the landlady won't let me stop it, she says it's bad for the works.

DR. SCHWÖRER. Well, give him his cup of strawberry tea, and you have my telephone number if anything happens. Goodnight, Madame Tchehov, goodnight. I'll be round at the usual time tomorrow.

(*The German band soars to a peak of banality, then cuts out; in the gap which it leaves there emerges the heavy tick-tocking of a clock.*)

OLGA. Now, Antosha, here's your strawberry tea.

TCHEHOV. Thank you, poppet.

OLGA. Sleepy?

TCHEHOV. I *am* rather.

OLGA. Tonight I have a feeling you're going to sleep *well*.

TCHEHOV. If I don't have dreams.

OLGA. You might have nice ones.

TCHEHOV. Nice dreams, Olga? No. My dreams these days are frightening. Pictures and voices from the past. And then there's that deep river.

OLGA. What deep river?

TCHEHOV. I told you, Olga, I told you. I've dreamt about it for years. It's like those rivers in Siberia. Great grey slippery stones on the bank; cold autumnal water; mist . . . mist over everything. It's all incredibly dismal and damp and I know that I have to cross it. Then I hear hooters in the mist. There are little tugs going up and down the river—

OLGA. You only dream that when your blanket falls off. Tonight I shall tuck you in *well*. . . . There! How's that?

TCHEHOV. Marvellous.

OLGA. Good. Now you're all fixed. Goodnight, Antosha darling. There's your little bell on the table. . . . Goodnight.

TCHEHOV. Goodnight, my practical wife.

(*A pause, then the hooter of a steamer.*)

TCHEHOV (*in his sleep*). The water looks so cold . . . and I can't see the other bank. . . .

(*The hooter again—forlornly. The voices which he now hears, have a strange—a dream—quality.*)

1ST CROUPIER. Faites vos jeux, messieurs et mesdames.

TCHEHOV. But who are the people in the boat?

FATHER. Fear God and you cannot go wrong.

2ND CROUPIER. Faites vos jeux, messieurs et mesdames.

(*Hooter.*)

TCHEHOV. The water looks so cold. . . . That's Nikolay in the boat, I fear he's getting consumption.

1ST CROUPIER. Les jeux sont faits. Rien ne va plus.

TCHEHOV. And that old man looks like Artem—Artem, my favourite actor.

ARTEM. 'They have gone . . . they have forgotten me. Never mind . . . I'll sit here a bit. . . . I'll be bound Leonid Andreyevitch hasn't put his fur coat on—'

TCHEHOV. He'll need his fur coat. It's cold on the water. . . . Isn't that Tolstoy sitting in the stern?

TOLSTOY. Anton Pavlovitch, don't be so feeble. You *must* have views on this subject.

(*Hooter.*)

TCHEHOV. Which subject?

1ST CROUPIER. Faites vos jeux, messieurs et mesdames.

FATHER. Fear God and you cannot go wrong.

BOY. Mother killed him. Give me another sugar-stick.

(*Hooter.*)

TCHEHOV. Which is the steamer for Odessa?

1ST CROUPIER. Les jeux sont faits. Rien ne va plus.

TCHEHOV. Which is the steamer for Odessa?

BOY. Mother killed him. Give me—

TCHEHOV (*urgently*). Which is the steamer for Odessa?

(*Long blast on the hooter: and it fades away as he wakes.*)

TCHEHOV (*crying out*). Olga!

(*He rings the hand-bell; she comes in.*)

OLGA. What is it, Antosha?

TCHEHOV. Which is the steamer for Odessa?

OLGA. What?

TCHEHOV. Nothing; I'm dreaming . . . .

OLGA. Do you feel all right?

TCHEHOV. Yes, I think so.

OLGA. You musn't dream like that. Was it the river again?

TCHEHOV. The river? Yes. The river. (*Pause.*) Olga!

OLGA. Yes?

TCHEHOV. I don't feel all right. I think I'd better have the doctor.

OLGA. The doctor!

TCHEHOV (*trying to laugh it off*). First time in my life I've asked for such a person. Being a doctor myself . . . .

OLGA. I'll ring him at once.

TCHEHOV. Don't go away, Olga.

OLGA. I'm just going down to the phone. Back in a second.

(*The clock fills in an interval.*)

OLGA (*in the foreground, but hushed*). But Dr. *Schwörer*—!

DR. SCHWÖRER. No, I'm afraid not . . . I saw this coming . . . but I didn't think that *tonight*—

OLGA. Are you *absolutely certain*?

DR. SCHWÖRER. Absolutely, Madame.

TCHEHOV (*from the background*). I know what you're saying over there—

OLGA (*switching on brightness*). Look, Antosha, look what the doctor's brought . . . Champagne!

TCHEHOV (*with sly seriousness*). Champagne! I know what that's for. (*With attempted jollity.*) Pour me a glass at once. . . . That's right; up to the brim.

DR. SCHWÖRER. Here you are, Dr. Tchehov.

TCHEHOV. Thank you, Herr Doktor, you're too kind, much too kind. . . . I know what you mean, you know; I am a doctor too. . . . Ich sterbe, Herr Doktor—that's good German, isn't it? Give me the glass. . . . Thank you . . . Olga, poppet, your health!

OLGA. Carefully, Antosha—

DR. SCHWÖRER. No, no, let him drink it to the bottom. . . .

That's the way I like to see a man drink.

(*The glass tinkles as it is put down.*)

TCHEHOV (*very feebly*). Good! . . . I hadn't tasted champagne for a long time.

DR. SCHWÖRER. Now, Madame, let him lie on his side . . . .

(*The clock, which we had forgotten, reasserts itself; dominating the death-bed.*)

DR. SCHWÖRER. No, do not speak to him now . . . . (*He drops his voice.*) What a wonderful smile!

(*The clock continues.*)

DR. SCHWÖRER. Wait, Madame, wait.

(*The clock continues, then suddenly breaks off and there is a gap of silence.*)

DR. SCHWÖRER. It is over, Madame.

OLGA. It is . . . over?

DR. SCHWÖRER. He died gently.

(*A slight pause and she speaks—contemplatively but decisively.*)

OLGA. Anton, doctor, did everything gently.

(*Silence and then the hooter of a steamer. Tchehov's voice is heard, speaking slowly in a great space.*)

TCHEHOV. Which is the steamer for Odessa? . . .

Where do we book our passage? Your passage and mine. For a future which *should* be happy.

THE NOSEBAG

a Russian folk story

TO

FRANCIS DILLON

CAST

The Nosebag was first broadcast in the B.B.C. Home Service on March 13th, 1944. The main parts were played as follows:

SOLDIER	ROY EMERTON
THIRD BEGGAR	BRYAN POWLEY*
LANDLORD	IVOR BARNARD
MARYA	MOLLY RANKIN*
CHAMBERLAIN	MALCOLM GRAEME
TSAR	PETER USTINOV
DEVIL CAPTAIN	HOWARD MARION-CRAWFORD
LITTLE DEVIL	JOHN GILPIN
DEATH	GLADYS YOUNG*

Production by the author.

NOTE: The square brackets on pages 111, 114, and 120 denote cuts in the broadcast (see also page 200).

INTRODUCTORY NOTE

The Nosebag is a direct and very simple dramatisation of a traditional Russian folk story which is usually entitled *The Soldier and Death*. Such programmes go well on the air, and, unlike satirical fantasies (see my two March Hare programmes), are usually popular with the listening public. It is surprising that more folk stories and fairy stories have not been dramatised for radio—outside the Children's Hour. There is, however, one notable pioneer in this field, Mr. Francis Dillon, whose wit, imagination, and sympathy with his original, have enabled him to make excellent radio plays out of Hans Andersen. These latter are more topical in feeling than *The Nosebag* and rightly so, as Hans Andersen was not of the folk; thus when Mr. Dillon in his version of *The Snow Queen* made the wicked Magicians atom-bomb scientists, he was simply developing Andersen's intention. But a folk-story proper, being timeless, cannot be so feasibly brought up to date *if* it is intended to retain its original flavour. In the characters of the Tsar and the Chamberlain (the latter my own interpolation) I hinted at modern types—with a touch of satire—but I did not tinker with the hero, and carefully avoided throughout both the temptation to cod and the shown-to-the-children manner. The 'folk' who made these stories were after all adults.

This broadcast suffered from not having special music (as I realised even more when in dramatising at a later date Apuleius' story of *The Golden Ass* I had the great advantage of special music by Mr. Antony Hopkins). As it was, I relied entirely both for linking and effects music on gramophone records, drawing on Liadow, Rimsky-Korsakov, Moussorgsky, Stravinsky *et al.* The mixture naturally failed to be a blend and the snippets of effects music failed to be duly functional.

The part of the Soldier was magnificently embodied by Roy

Emerton whose death during the last year deprived his profession of a very rare personality. Having a deep, very powerful voice which was naturally rough but without any 'accent', he was peculiarly suited to a part which had to be so genuinely earthy.

THE NOSEBAG

ANNOUNCER. The Nosebag! The programme that follows is a traditional Russian folk-tale. The story itself is fantastic but the hero is a true Russian peasant. We hope you will all find something in: The Nosebag.

(Introductory music.)

SOLDIER. Damn the sergeant! Damn the officer! Damn the Colonel! Damn the General! Who do they think they are to do such a thing to me? After twenty-five years of service. Out on my neck and the wind is cold and the steppes are wide and the years are empty. A discharged soldier that nobody wants. Twenty-five years of service to God and the Great Tsar. And now discharged . . . discharged! And nothing to show for it all but three dry biscuits. Three . . . dry . . . biscuits. Well. It's a long road; I'd best be moving. Left—left—left right left; left—left—

1ST BEGGAR. Soldier! Soldier! Stop!

SOLDIER. What's up, father?

(Pause.)

No, I've got no money.

1ST BEGGAR. No money, soldier. Food! I have sixty years of age and little breath in my body. Hunger is always with me and—

SOLDIER. Hunger? Take him away. And take this biscuit too.

1ST BEGGAR. May the good God bless you, soldier.

SOLDIER. Aye, may the good God bless me. Two . . . dry . . . biscuits. Left—left—left right—

2ND BEGGAR. Soldier!

SOLDIER. What do *you* want?

2ND BEGGAR. Food, soldier, for the love of God. I have seventy years of age and—

SOLDIER. No flesh on your bones, eh. This won't help you much but—

2ND BEGGAR. A biscuit! A biscuit! May the good God reward you.

SOLDIER. In the next life maybe. One . . . dry . . . biscuit. Well, well, a Russian soldier cannot drown in water or burn in fire. This is a long road but who knows whether—

3RD BEGGAR. Soldier!

(*The Third Beggar speaks with a serenity lacking in his predecessors.*)

SOLDIER. A third old rag-and-bones!

3RD BEGGAR. Soldier, forgive me for stopping you. I am an old man—older than you can guess—I have not eaten today, yesterday I dined on birch-bark—

SOLDIER. I've done that in my time. I know what you'd like. See this?

Not so fast, greybeard. Suppose we break it in two?

3RD BEGGAR. Just as you will, soldier.

SOLDIER. Seems more sense to halve it. All the same . . . .

3RD BEGGAR. All the same?

SOLDIER. Your brother beggars got a biscuit each; it don't seem fair that—Here!

3RD BEGGAR. All for me?

SOLDIER. Aye, beggar. I never liked biscuits anyway.

3RD BEGGAR. I thank you, soldier. Now it is my turn. Tell me how I can help you.

SOLDIER. You! Help me! God bless you, beggar, you couldn't help a fly.

3RD BEGGAR. You think not? Have faith. What would you like?

SOLDIER. Nothing, old fellow, nothing. Leastways, maybe, for a keepsake—you haven't a pack of cards, have you?

3RD BEGGAR. Cards? Here.

SOLDIER. Upon my soul, brand-new!

3RD BEGGAR. Whomsoever you play with, using these cards you will win.

SOLDIER. Eh?

3RD BEGGAR. And here . . . is something else.

SOLDIER. What's that? A nosebag!

3RD BEGGAR. A nosebag.

SOLDIER. A nosebag! What in the name of—

3RD BEGGAR. Soldier, mark what I say. You have been good to me, I will be good to you.

SOLDIER. Aye, but a nosebag without a horse—

3RD BEGGAR. You can have horses and all if you want. As you go on by this road, whatever you see that you fancy, be it beast, bird or fish—just you hold out this bag and open the mouth of it so and call out 'Beast or bird! Jump in here in my nosebag.' And mark my words, they will.

SOLDIER. Ha! Ha! Ha! Ha! Ha! That's a good story if ever I—

3RD BEGGAR. A good story is a true story. You do not know who I am, soldier—

SOLDIER. Who *are* you?

3RD BEGGAR. I leave you to guess, soldier. But make a good use of my gifts. Farewell now. God bless you.

(*A balalaika fades up; introducing an Inn crowded with noisy peasants.*)

1ST PEASANT. Come on, landlord. Vodka on credit.

LANDLORD. Nothing on credit, friend. Not in these days.

1ST PEASANT. Stingy old cheese-paring—

MARYA. No, he's right. In these days a body has got to—

1ST PEASANT. A body has got to have vodka.

2ND PEASANT. Aye, that's right. Folks won't come to no good unless—

LANDLORD. Folks won't come to no good unless they work, I tell you.

2ND PEASANT. A body can't work without drink. And food too, o'course. When I remember the old days—

ALL. A-a-ah!

1ST PEASANT. Rivers of brown beer!

2ND PEASANT. Armies of roast geese!

SOLDIER (*entering*). Who wants roast geese?

LANDLORD. Come in, soldier. Sit down. But, if you want drink, you must pay.

SOLDIER. I said: Who wants roast goose?

MARYA. Who wants it! Hark ye, soldier, you look like a stranger here and a joke's a joke but—

SOLDIER. See what I've got in my hand?

MARYA. A nosebag. What about it?

SOLDIER. Well, it looks full, don't it? Guess what I've got inside.

2ND PEASANT. *I* know . . . Hay!

VOICES. That's right. Hay.

SOLDIER. Well, look here.

One!

Two!!

Three!!!

LANDLORDS. The saints preserve us! Geese!

ALL. Geese! Geese! Geese!

SOLDIER. Three wild geese. Landlord, take 'em. The first you can roast for my supper, the second you can change for vodka—

2ND PEASANT. Ooh, won't he be drunk!

SOLDIER. And the third you can keep as payment.

LANDLORD. Upon my soul—

SOLDIER. Is that fair or isn't it?

LANDLORD. Fair? Of course it's fair, sir. Now, sir, if you'd like to sit here, sir—

SOLDIER. You needn't sir me and I won't sit here. Give me that big table and lay a place for all.

MARYA. What do you mean?

SOLDIER. When I have luck I share it. Sit you down, folks.

1ST PEASANT. Me?

2ND PEASANT. Me?

SOLDIER. All of you.

(*Cheers.*)

2ND PEASANT. All of us except Marya. She has to do the cooking.

MARYA. Aye and it'll take time.

2ND PEASANT. All the more time for drinking.

SOLDIER. Aye, and for music. Landlord!

LANDLORD. Yes, sir?

SOLDIER. Give us some music, can't you?

LANDLORD. Music, sir, but—

SOLDIER (*authoritatively*). Music!

(*The balalaika strikes up.*)

SOLDIER. That's more like it.

(*A pause; then he puts an idle question.*)

SOLDIER. What's that big house yonder out of the window?

(*The balalaika breaks off abruptly; the peasants whisper.*)

SOLDIER. Why has the music stopped?

LANDLORD. Because of what you said, sir.

MARYA. The music always stops when a body mentions that.

SOLDIER. Mentions what?

2ND PEASANT. The house outside the window.

SOLDIER. Why! A man can mention a house.

LANDLORD. Aye, sir, but that is the Tsar's palace.

SOLDIER. Pah! A man can mention a palace.

LANDLORD. Aye, sir, but this is a haunted palace.

(*The peasants murmur endorsement.*)

SOLDIER. Haunted?

LANDLORD. Aye, soldier, by devils.

1ST PEASANT. Aye, a regular pack of 'em. Every shape and size and—

MARYA. See them windows, soldier? Bain't a whole pane of glass in 'em.

1ST PEASANT. They meets there every night. Horrible goings-on.

SOLDIER. They do?

LANDLORD. They do indeed, sir. Every night at midnight in they comes a-growling and screeching—you can hear 'em from over here.

MARYA. Playing cards and dicing and—

SOLDIER. What does the Tsar do?

LANDLORD. Tsar? He ain't put his foot in there for over a dozen years.

2ND PEASANT. That's right. No one can spend a night in that there palace and live.

SOLDIER. Is that so? Where can I find this Tsar?

(*The peasants express alarm.*)

LANDLORD. He lives in the next parish but what do you—

SOLDIER. Never you mind. Fill up your glasses, friends. (*decisively*) I shall call on your Tsar tomorrow.

(*Court music leads to the Court—and to Tomorrow.*)

CHAMBERLAIN (*approaching*). Your most Imperial Majesty.

TSAR. Yes, yes, what the deuce is it now?

CHAMBERLAIN. A discharged soldier is waiting without at the gate.

TSAR. A discharged soldier? Go and discharge him again.

CHAMBERLAIN. But your Imperial—

TSAR. I will *not* have my mornings disturbed by men of the people. There *is* such a thing as autocracy. Why, in my father's time—

SOLDIER (*entering*). Good morning. Are you the Tsar?

TSAR. What!

CHAMBERLAIN. Who let that man in here?

SOLDIER. I let myself in, master. I've got business with—

TSAR. Call in the guard and clap this fellow in gaol.

SOLDIER. In gaol, eh? (*Slyly*) Why not the haunted palace?

TSAR. The haunted—What do you want, you scum, with the haunted palace?

SOLDIER (*dead-pan*). I want to see them devils.

TSAR. Why? They'd tear you to pieces, man.

SOLDIER. You think so?

TSAR. I know so. Other people have tried this game before. And not just trash like you. Well set-up young fellows with blue blood in their veins but it was all the same. When we sent round in the morning all we found was their bones. (*With gusto.*) And the ivory floors were red with their blood.

SOLDIER. Red? Why not blue?

TSAR. I believe it *was* blue. But as I was saying—

SOLDIER. What will you give me if I get rid of them devils?

TSAR. Give you? What did we offer 'em last time?

CHAMBERLAIN. I do not remember, Your Majesty. It was a large sum.

SOLDIER. Well, give me a large sum. Now where's the key?

CHAMBERLAIN. What do you mean, boor? His Majesty has not as yet consented to—

TSAR. Give him the key, give him the key. There you are, soldier. Let yourself in tonight and we'll fetch you out tomorrow.

CHAMBERLAIN (*smoothly*). His Majesty means your bones.

(*Ghost music creeps up and continues while the Soldier walks round inspecting.*)

SOLDIER. So this is the haunted palace. Fancy carvings. Ivory. Marble. Must have cost a bit. Draughty though—and don't it smell? That'll be all this muck on the floors. Devils done that, I reckon. Bones, feathers—(*he laughs but not happily*) might be a barnyard. Lucky the moon shines in, I can find me a place to sit. (*He speaks slowly, settling himself.*) Time for a nice smoke before it comes on to midnight.

(*Music and Wind. A clock begins striking midnight, then is drowned in jabbering and screeching.*)

DEVIL CAPTAIN. Devils! You all here?

VOICES. Aye, aye, Captain.

DEVIL CAPTAIN. Good. Orders for tonight are simple. Palace to be haunted from end to end as usual. Every devil to be on his worst behaviour. Is that in disorder?

VOICES. Aye, sir.

DEVIL CAPTAIN. Right. In you go!

(*Music swells up, as the Devils cheer.*)

1ST DEVIL. Hugger and mugger, pell and mell,
Here we come the devils from Hell.

2ND DEVIL. Fire and brimstone, bug and nit,
Here we come from the burning pit.

3RD DEVIL. Horn and dewclaw, blood and malice,
Here we come to the Tsar's palace.

4TH DEVIL. Cloven hoof and burning bill,
This big devil is out to kill.

LITTLE DEVIL. Shining tusk and twining tail,
This little devil is . . .
is . . .
is . . .
Oh, I do want a rhyme!

DEVIL CAPTAIN. Devils! Halt! (*The music ends.*) This is no time for rhymes. What do I see at the far end of the hall?

1ST DEVIL. A man!

2ND DEVIL. A man!

3RD DEVIL. A man!

4TH DEVIL. A man!

LITTLE DEVIL. A live one!

DEVIL CAPTAIN. Ahoy there, man!

SOLDIER (*distant*). Ahoy there, devils!

DEVIL CAPTAIN. Come up here.

SOLDIER (*distant*). Com-ing.

4TH DEVIL. Ph-e-ew! Now for some fun.

2ND DEVIL. Not seen one of these in a twelvemonth.

LITTLE DEVIL. Aw, why did I leave my pitchfork at home?

(*The devils growl in anticipation.*)

DEVIL CAPTAIN. Silence there. I'll handle this business. No one to act till I give the order. I want no biting, scratching, pronging, eating-up or other molestation, until such time as—

SOLDIER (*joining them*). Hullo there, Scaly.

DEVIL CAPTAIN. Welcome, soldier, to our little party. What can we do to amuse you?

SOLDIER. I'm amused already. Ha! Ha! Ha! Such a funny-looking bunch I never in my life—Ha! Ha! Ha!—

(*The devils hiss at him.*)

DEVIL CAPTAIN. I beg your pardon. I merely wanted to know what are your favourite pastimes. Dancing? Skittles? Knucklebones? Cards?

SOLDIER. Cards.

DEVIL CAPTAIN. Excellent. Now take a seat here at this table and—Who's got a pack?

SOLDIER. I have.

DEVIL CAPTAIN. A new pack, eh?

SOLDIER. Somebody gave it me. Want me to deal?

DEVIL CAPTAIN. Go ahead.

(*The devils scratch on the table and jabber.*)

DEVILS. Yub-a-yub-a-yub-a-yub-a-yub-a-yub-a-yub . . . .

SOLDIER. Now then. Turn 'em up.

1ST DEVIL. [Seven of Hearts.

2ND DEVIL. Four of Clubs.

3RD DEVIL. Knave of Clubs.

4TH DEVIL. Ten of Diamonds.

DEVIL CAPTAIN. Queen of Spades.

SOLDIER. Ace of Diamonds.

DEVILS. Urrr-urrr-urrr-urrr-urrr . . . .

SOLDIER (*very calmly*). Your gold, please. Your deal, Scaly.

DEVIL CAPTAIN. Thank you.

LITTLE DEVIL. Hee-hee-hee. Now we'll see some play.]

(*Short passage of music to cover another round.*)

SOLDIER. Your gold please.

(*Ditto.*)

SOLDIER. Your gold please.

(*Ditto.*)

SOLDIER. Your gold please.

(*The music ends. The devils are very angry.*)

DEVILS. Urrr-urrr-urrr-urrr-urrr . . . .

DEVIL CAPTAIN. Extraordinary, quite extraordinary. Skraglitch!

LITTLE DEVIL. Here, sir.

DEVIL CAPTAIN. Run back to Hell and fetch some more money.

LITTLE DEVIL. Yes, sir. How much, sir?

DEVIL CAPTAIN. Every ounce you can carry. And don't go dropping it in space.

LITTLE DEVIL. No, sir; I won't, sir.

DEVIL CAPTAIN. Well, soldier, your luck's been quite phenomenal. (*The devils growl.*) But, as I always say, he who laughs last—Ah, Skraglitch! Put it down here.

LITTLE DEVIL. Pretty good time, eh, captain? I didn't drop none either.

DEVIL CAPTAIN. Put the money down and stop talking. Now then, friends, whose deal is it?

(*The devils scratch the table and jabber as before. Short passage of music.*)

SOLDIER. Your gold, please.

(*The music ends abruptly. This is too much.*)

SOLDIER. What, are you all cleaned out? Looks as if the game is over.

DEVIL CAPTAIN. On the contrary, soldier, the game is about to begin. Devils! Where are your pitchforks?

(*Hubbub.*)

LITTLE DEVIL. Aw, why did I leave mine at home!

DEVIL CAPTAIN. Now then, before we destroy him—Aren't you afraid, soldier?

SOLDIER. Afraid? What of? A Russian soldier cannot drown in—

DEVIL CAPTAIN. Yes, yes, yes, I know that proverb: A Russian soldier can't burn in water. (*The devils laugh.*) But, Russian soldier or no Russian soldier, you've cheated at cards and you're going to pay for it.

(*The devils growl, warming up.*)

SOLDIER. Stand back devils. See this?

DEVILS. A nosebag?

LITTLE DEVIL. A dirty old, empty old nosebag.

SOLDIER. Dirty. Maybe. Empty? We'll see about that.

(*More growling.*)

SOLDIER (*with sudden authority*). Devils—in the name of God—in with you into my nosebag!

(*Screams. Music.*)

SOLDIER. That's right. One—two—three—four—five—six—seven—eight—nine—ten—eleven—twelve—thirteen . . . .

(*His voice is drowned in music—which passes away like the night.*)

CHAMBERLAIN. Your Imperial Majesty. Your morning vodka.

TSAR. Morning already! What's going on in the world?

CHAMBERLAIN. Nothing new, Your Majesty. Except the soldier, of course.

TSAR. Soldier?

CHAMBERLAIN. The one that slept last night in the haunted palace.

TSAR. Oh, yes, yes—Have they fetched his bones yet?

CHAMBERLAIN. No, Your Imperial—

TSAR. If not, why not?

CHAMBERLAIN. The Captain of the Guards reports that he called at the palace at dawn but there were no bones to be found.

TSAR. Not even bones. Poor fellow!

CHAMBERLAIN. The odd thing is, Your Majesty, a report has just been received that a soldier of similar appearance was seen an hour or two back calling on the village blacksmith.

TSAR. On the village blacksmith? Why?

CHAMBERLAIN. He is said to have been carrying a nosebag.

TSAR. A what?

CHAMBERLAIN. A nosebag, Your Majesty. Rather a common object.

TSAR. Hmph. What are the other facts in the case?

CHAMBERLAIN. No other facts, Your Majesty. Merely a soldier, a nosebag, a blacksmith.

(*A pause.*)

SOLDIER. Now then, smith. You and your mate get hold of this bag and lay it there on the anvil.

1ST SMITH. Right.

2ND SMITH. Right.

1ST SMITH. Oh, heavy!

2ND SMITH. Heavy. Aye. What you got in her, soldier?

SOLDIER. Never you mind. Just lay that bag on the anvil and beat it hard the pair of you—in the ancient manner of smiths.

1ST SMITH. [Right, let me get my breath. I'm sweating already with the weight of her.

2ND SMITH. The devil must be in that nosebag.

LITTLE DEVIL (*muffled*). You're right, father. We are!

1ST SMITH. What's that?

2ND SMITH. The saints preserve us!

SOLDIER. The saints will preserve you. Get on with the job. Lay to.]

(*A rhythmical clanging; the devils shriek.*)

SOLDIER. This is music, this is. Bling, blong, bling, blong. Harder, my friends. harder!

(*The clanging rises to a peak, then slowly fades away. The devils are back in Hell—but very tired.*)

4TH DEVIL. Ooh—I never thought we'd see this place again.

2ND DEVIL. Smell the good old pitch and—How are your bones, brothers?

1ST DEVIL. Broken every one of 'em. If he hadn't let us out when he did, I think I'd have—

LITTLE DEVIL. Where's the Captain?

3RD DEVIL. That's right. Where's the Captain?

2ND DEVIL. Don't say he's still back there.

4TH DEVIL. He may be, you know. He was at the bottom of the bag.

LITTLE DEVIL. Poor old Captain! He was a bit strict sometimes but—

1ST DEVIL. Talk of the devil! Here he comes now.

ALL. Welcome, Captain. Welcome back to Hell.

DEVIL CAPTAIN (*breathless*). Give me a chair, someone.

4TH DEVIL. What happened, Captain, what happened?

DEVIL CAPTAIN. Keep this under your horns. That blest soldier —when he unbuckled the bag—I was the last, you know—well, it's really all too humiliating—

LITTLE DEVIL. Go on, Captain, tell us.

DEVIL CAPTAIN. The fellow caught me by the tail and before he would let me go—a strong fellow, that soldier—he got me to sign a contract.

DEVILS. A contract!

DEVIL CAPTAIN. Yes, I know, it's unheard of. But what could I do? I—

4TH DEVIL. You didn't promise nothing, did you?

DEVIL CAPTAIN. I'm afraid I did. I—

LITTLE DEVIL. Well, you can break it, Captain.

DEVIL CAPTAIN. That's enough from you. A devil's promise is a gentleman's promise. ('*That's right*' *say the adult devils.*) I have undertaken to serve that soldier whenever he chooses to call on me.

2ND DEVIL. Umph! That's hard.

DEVIL CAPTAIN. Hard, my good man? It's degrading. But I'll get my own back. If ever that soldier fellow fancies a billet in hell—Sergeant!

4TH DEVIL. Here, sir.

DEVIL CAPTAIN. From this day forward double the guard. Have all the gates reinforced. Lookouts on every turret.

4TH DEVIL. Yes, sir.

DEVIL CAPTAIN. On the first report of a soldier with a nosebag, ring the tocsin and man the ramparts.

4TH DEVIL. Yes, sir.

DEVIL CAPTAIN. He laughs longest who laughs last. That soldier may think himself clever, he may have the entrée to all the kingdoms of earth, but he won't have an entrée here.

LITTLE DEVIL. What's an entrée, Captain?

DEVIL CAPTAIN. No, he won't; not in a billion years.

2ND DEVIL. That'll learn him. Maybe now he's saying to himself he's happy. What a mistake! Happy!

(*Idyllic music flowers up, covering a passage of time.*)

SOLDIER. Oh how happy I am. All in the world that I want except a wife.

(*Music.*)

SOLDIER. My dear wife! What joy it is to be married. All in the world that I want—except a son.

(*Music.*)

SOLDIER. More vodka there! More vodka! Raise your glasses, brothers. We will drink to the health of my son who was born today.

(*The music comes to a happy close.*)

TSAR. Chamberlain, what's the news?

CHAMBERLAIN. No news, Your Imperial Majesty.

TSAR. How is my good friend, the discharged soldier?

CHAMBERLAIN. Nothing new about him. He's just happy, as usual.

TSAR. Rich as ever?

CHAMBERLAIN. Yes, Your Im—

TSAR. Wife as lovely as ever?

CHAMBERLAIN. So they say, Your Majesty.

TSAR. And how is his little boy?

CHAMBERLAIN. According to the Court News he is five years old tomorrow. And never yet, Your Majesty, never yet had a cold.

TSAR. Never had a cold! Bah! I don't believe it. Why, I was swaddled in velvet and I had a cold in the cradle—

(*sneezes*)

Yes—and I've got one now.

CHAMBERLAIN. I am more than grieved to hear it.

(*sneezes*)

Your Majesty will perceive that I have a cold myself.

TSAR (*snaps at him*). Then don't come near me. Yours might be something worse.

CHAMBERLAIN. Something worse, Your Majesty? I can assure you it's—

TSAR. My German doctor tells me there's plague about.

CHAMBERLAIN. Yes, Your Majesty. Two or three thousand cases. But that begins with boils.

TSAR. You got any boils?

CHAMBERLAIN. Your Majesty!

TSAR. All right, all right. One can't be too careful though. The doctor tells me these boils spring up overnight. And once that appears, you're done for.

(*The Soldier's Wife is heard—calling out as she approaches.*)

WIFE. Husband! . . . Husband! . . . Husband!

SOLDIER. What is it now, wife of my heart? Have you lost your pearls again?

WIFE. No. It's little Ivan. I've found a boil on his neck.

SOLDIER. A boil? . . . A boil. . . . Not the . . . the plague?

WIFE. I have sent for the Tsar's doctor. He is looking him over now.

SOLDIER (*slowly; unprecedentedly serious*). If it was to be the plague . . . .

DOCTOR (*approaching*). Gnädige Frau. Be so good as to send for some water.

WIFE. Water? He needs water?

DOCTOR. No, it is I who need it. To wash my hands, verstehen. In contact with fatal diseases I make it my practice to—

SOLDIER. What do you mean—fatal diseases?

DOCTOR. Your son has the plague. (*The Wife exclaims in agony.*) I give him twenty-four hours. Will you please send for that water? So. And a towel.

(*Music punctuates the following.*)

SOLDIER. Dead within twenty-four hours.

. . . .

Within twelve hours.

. . . .

Within six hours.

. . . .

Dead within three hours.

. . . .

Within two hours.

. . . .

Within ONE hour.

. . . .

(*The music wilts away.*)

WIFE (*broken*). Husband! Can you do nothing?

SOLDIER. I'm not a doctor. What the devil can *I*—Eh! 'What the *devil*'? Where's that contract gone to?

WIFE. What contract? Why are you searching in the mattress?

SOLDIER. Here it is, here it is! Leave me alone, my love, time is short.

WIFE. But, husband—

SOLDIER. Leave me alone, I say.

WIFE. But I must nurse Ivan.

SOLDIER. I will see to Ivan. Go. Go out of the room.

WIFE (*submitting to a forlorn hope*). Very well then.

(*The door closes.*)

SOLDIER. Now then. Quickly. Where's that cheat of a devil?

DEVIL CAPTAIN (*popping up*). Cheat! . . . Who says that I am a cheat?

SOLDIER. All right. You prove you're not. See this contract?

DEVIL CAPTAIN (*ungraciously*). What do you want me to do?

SOLDIER. Look over there. In the cot.

(*Pause while the devil moves over. His voice sounds further off.*)

DEVIL CAPTAIN (*matter-of-fact*). Hm! Your son looks ill.

SOLDIER. The plague, devil, the plague!

DEVIL CAPTAIN. Want me to cure him?

SOLDIER. Can you?

DEVIL CAPTAIN. That remains to be seen. I have something here in my pocket. This glass. Fill it with water.

(A sound of bubbling water.)

DEVIL CAPTAIN. Thank you.

Now then; we hold this glass over the patient's bed. Come here and stand by me. Look in this glass and tell me what you can see.

SOLDIER. See, devil? . . . Nothing. Nothing but bubbles, that is.

DEVIL CAPTAIN. Those bubbles will soon settle. Keep on looking. Well?

SOLDIER. Bubbles; only bubbles.

DEVIL CAPTAIN. Go on. Go on looking.

SOLDIER. Ah!

DEVIL CAPTAIN. Yes?

SOLDIER. I see . . . I see . . . I see my son in his cot.

DEVIL CAPTAIN. Yes?

SOLDIER. And I see the figure of a woman standing beside him.

DEVIL CAPTAIN. Know who that is, soldier? That is Death.

SOLDIER. Death!

DEVIL CAPTAIN. Of course. Where is she standing?

SOLDIER. Where?

DEVIL CAPTAIN. At his head or his feet?

SOLDIER. His feet.

DEVIL CAPTAIN. That's all we need to know. If Death stands at his feet your boy will survive.

SOLDIER. Thank God!

DEVIL CAPTAIN. Now if she were at his head—ha! ha!—nothing could save him, soldier.

Here, take this water and pour it over the child.

CHILD. Ouch!

DEVIL CAPTAIN. You see? He has come to.

SOLDIER. Ah, God be praised for this—

DEVIL CAPTAIN. *God* be praised, eh? Well, anything else you want?

SOLDIER. No, devil. Unless . . . .

DEVIL CAPTAIN. Unless what?

SOLDIER. Would you give me that glass of yours?

DEVIL CAPTAIN. Oh no! Oh no you don't.

SOLDIER. Go on, devil. If you give me that glass, I'll release you from this here contract.

DEVIL CAPTAIN. Ah, that's different. Hand me the contract and I'll—Thank you.

(*A noise of tearing parchment.*)

DEVIL CAPTAIN. Goodbye, soldier. You know how to use the glass?

SOLDIER. Aye. From this day on *I'm* setting up for a doctor.

(*Funereal music creeps in, leads to the Chamberlain's sickbed.*)

CHAMBERLAIN. [Where's that doctor? Where's that doctor? Didn't you take him my message?

MAIDSERVANT. I'm sorry, master. He says, if you've got the plague, he's attending no more cases.

CHAMBERLAIN. The damned German! Isn't there—

MAIDSERVANT. He says, master, that all that remains for you is to say your prayers and die. But if you was to ask *me* . . . .

CHAMBERLAIN. What? Go on, I'm asking you.

MAIDSERVANT. I'd say my prayers and send for that discharged soldier.

CHAMBERLAIN (*with distaste*). The discharged soldier? Why?

MAIDSERVANT. Folks do say that he has a cure for the plague. He's cured a few already. Boyars, generals and that. Does it all with a glass.

SOLDIER (*entering*). Aye. With a glass. Like this.

MAIDSERVANT. Well! Talk of the devil!

SOLDIER. No, you don't; don't talk of the devil to me. (*cheerily*) Now then, Chamberlain, want to be cured?

CHAMBERLAIN. What's that medicine?

SOLDIER. Water, only water. And I hold it above you so. Now come here you and tell me what you can see.

MAIDSERVANT. See? . . . I can see bubbles.

SOLDIER. Go on looking. Now?

MAIDSERVANT. I see the master lying on his bed.

CHAMBERLAIN. Hmph! You don't have to look in a glass to—

SOLDIER. Hsh! Anything else?

MAIDSERVANT. Aye. A kind of a woman—

SOLDIER. That's not a woman; that's Death.

(The Chamberlain moans with horror.)

MAIDSERVANT. Death?

SOLDIER. At his head or his feet?

MAIDSERVANT. At his, er—now, now, now, I can't see if you joggle the glass—She's standing right at his feet.

SOLDIER. Here's a cold douche for you, Chamberlain.

CHAMBERLAIN. Ow! What do you mean by—

SOLDIER. I'll send you the bill in the morning.

(Funereal music, as before.)

DOCTOR. A boil! So? The plague! Call the lawyers and I'll make my will.

SOLDIER (*entering*). Your will will keep, Herr Doktor. Want to be cured?

DOCTOR. Who let *you* in, quack?

SOLDIER. 'Want to be cured?', I said.

DOCTOR. No one can cure this plague. I am a doctor, I know.

SOLDIER (*sardonically, moving off*). Well, if you know . . . .

DOCTOR. Where are you going?

SOLDIER. Well, I thought as I'm not welcome—

DOCTOR. What is this cure of yours?

SOLDIER. It's simple, Herr Doktor, but it's costly.

DOCTOR. What is your fee?

SOLDIER. If I cure you, as I can, you must resign to me—(*he pauses to get his effect*) your post as the Tsar's physician.

DOCTOR. As the Tsar's—but no, no, no! I will not give up my post. Besides it is ridiculous. You as the Tsar's physician! No, no, no! A million times no. A thousand times no. A hundred times no. Ten times no . . .].

(Funereal music as before.)

CHAMBERLAIN. Send for the Tsar's physician. The Tsar is ill unto death.

SOLDIER. You need not send, Chamberlain. News travels fast these days; I travel faster. Just fill me this glass with water and—

TSAR. Who's that? The discharged soldier?

SOLDIER. The Tsar's physician, Your Imperial Majesty.

TSAR. Thank God you are here. You can cure me?

CHAMBERLAIN. He cured *me*, Your Majesty.

TSAR. That's nothing to do with it.

CHAMBERLAIN. He has also cured hundreds of boyars, dozens of generals and—

TSAR. Hold your tongue. Have you filled his glass with water?

CHAMBERLAIN. Yes, Your Imperial—

TSAR. Well, then, let him get on with it.

SOLDIER. Chamberlain, stand by me. Look in this glass and look very carefully. What do you see?

CHAMBERLAIN. Bubbles.

SOLDIER (*smugly echoing him*). Bubbles.

CHAMBERLAIN. A figure.

SOLDIER. A figure.

CHAMBERLAIN. The Tsar in his bed.

SOLDIER. The Tsar in his bed.

CHAMBERLAIN. And another figure.

SOLDIER. Death.

CHAMBERLAIN. Death! Dear me, is that—

SOLDIER. Death standing at his feet.

CHAMBERLAIN. But no, soldier, no.

SOLDIER (*shocked*). What!

CHAMBERLAIN. Look in your own glass. It's Death standing at his head.

SOLDIER. At his what? . . . What! . . . (*resigning himself*) Aye. Death standing at his head.

(*Pause.*)

TSAR. Come on, come on; I'm not cured yet.

SOLDIER (*quietly*). You never will be, Your Imperial Majesty.

TSAR. What's that? What do you mean, man?

SOLDIER. You have three hours left to live.

TSAR. You liar!

SOLDIER. No, your Imperial—

TSAR. Did you not cure the boyars?

SOLDIER. Aye.

TSAR. And the generals?

SOLDIER. Aye.

TSAR. And my Chamberlain here?

CHAMBERLAIN. Aye—Yes, I mean.

TSAR. And you refuse to cure me!

SOLDIER. I do not refuse, I—

TSAR. You are a traitor. I'll have you beheaded at once.

CHAMBERLAIN. Shall I pass on the order, Your Majesty?

TSAR. Yes. Behead him at once and—

(*A female voice cuts in—very rarefied and formal.*)

DEATH. I only bargained for one. Now it seems there'll be two.

TSAR. What's that? Who's talking?

DEATH. One by the plague and one by the block.

CHAMBERLAIN. Cherchez la femme, Your Majesty, cherchez la—

SOLDIER. Hsh, you! Look in this glass, can't you? There's the one that's doing the talking. Death! Hi, Death! That you?

DEATH. Aye, soldier. Greetings.

SOLDIER. You are waiting to take the Tsar?

DEATH. I am, soldier.

SOLDIER. Supposing now . . . supposing . . . .

DEATH. Supposing what?

SOLDIER. You are a person of honour. You only bargained for one. Well now . . . .

DEATH. Yes?

SOLDIER (*taking the plunge*). Instead of the Tsar, why don't you take me?

DEATH. You, soldier?

SOLDIER. What's the odds? He's going to behead me anyway. Give the old pig his life and take me instead.

DEATH. Do you want it that way?

TSAR. We do!

SOLDIER. Nobody asked you. Aye. I want it that way. But give me just three hours more. Then I'll have time to get home and say farewell to my family.

DEATH. So be it, soldier. I release my claims on the Tsar and you shall have three hours more. I shall be there at your bedside.

(*Music punctuates the following.*)

SOLDIER. Farewell, my friends.

. . . .

Farewell, Ivan my son.

. . . .

Farewell, my beloved wife.

. . . .

DEATH. Your time is up, soldier.

(*The music ends; the Soldier's time is up.*)

SOLDIER (*feebly*). That you, Death? Where are you?

DEATH. Your eyes are dim. You have only three minutes left to live in the bright world. So hurry, soldier, I'm waiting. What are you doing, rummaging under the pillow?

SOLDIER. Looking for something. A locket.

DEATH. A locket? Hm. Always the same story. Well, find it quickly and—

SOLDIER. Here she is.

DEATH. That's not a locket.

SOLDIER. What is it then?

DEATH. Why that thing's a . . . .

SOLDIER. What?

DEATH. Why, that's just an old nosebag.

SOLDIER. You sure about that?

DEATH. Of course I am. Enough of this nonsense; I've got other engagements—

SOLDIER. One thing at a time, Mistress Death. If this is a nosebag —jump into it.

(*Musical effect, representing the Nosebag Trick.*)

PEASANT. Hey, soldier. What have you got in that nosebag.

SOLDIER. Never you mind. Is this the way to the forest?

PEASANT. Yonder's the forest ahead of you. That bag of yours looks heavy.

SOLDIER. It *is* heavy, my brother.

PEASANT. It's cold in that forest, soldier.

SOLDIER. Cold? (*gleefully*) The colder the better.

(*Music and wind. Here is the forest.*)

SOLDIER (*grunting from his efforts*). Now then—the bitter aspen— the very top of it—the topmost twig—fasten her well. (*triumphantly*) Goodbye, nosebag. Goodbye, Death. Looks as if from now on folks won't die any more.

(*The forest music recedes slowly into Ancient History.*)

TSAR. Extraordinary thing, Chamberlain. Nobody's died here lately. Noticed that in your rounds?

CHAMBERLAIN. How could I not, Your Majesty? The bishop says it's a scandal.

TSAR. No more burial fees, eh?

CHAMBERLAIN. No, Your Majesty; it's serious.

(*Passage of music: the Non-Dying Era progresses.*)

CHAMBERLAIN. Your Majesty, this really is serious.

TSAR. What's it now, Chamberlain?

CHAMBERLAIN. The census has just come in.

TSAR. Yes? What of it?

CHAMBERLAIN. It proves beyond a doubt that your kingdom is over-populated.

TSAR. Is it? Why?

CHAMBERLAIN. Because, Your Majesty, none of us ever die.

TSAR. When was the last death?

CHAMBERLAIN. Oh years ago, Your Majesty.

TSAR. Years? You mean decades!

CHAMBERLAIN. Your Majesty is always right. I ought to have said decades.

(*Another passage of music*).

SOLDIER. Well, well, well, lovely weather today! Just the right day to have taken this trip to the city. Beautiful blue sky, everyone ought to be happy. But they're not, you know, they're not. Look at that old woman blowing about in the wind—and there's hardly a wind to speak of—just like she was a straw. My word, that's an old woman. It's almost time she died.

OLD WOMAN (*croaking with age and misery*). You took the words out of my mouth, discharged soldier. Almost time I died! That time has come and gone. Long, long years ago. And ever since then my life—if you call it life—is an agony. And you know whose fault that is. The day that you put Death in the nosebag, I had no more than an hour to live in the white world. All I want is rest and it's you who's kept it from me.

SOLDIER. I'm sorry, mother.

OLD WOMAN. Sorry! Do you know what you've done, soldier? You've committed an unforgivable sin. And there's other folk like me. Have you ever thought about that?

SOLDIER. No, I can't say I—

OLD WOMAN. Then you'd better think now. And if you can undo what you've done—maybe you can't—

(*Suddenly converted, he interrupts her.*)

SOLDIER. No? . . . Maybe I can.

(*Back to the Forest. Wind and music.*)

SOLDIER (*shouting*). Death! Death! . . . Where's that bitter aspen? Ah, here we are.

Death! Hey, Death, are you alive?

DEATH (*distant and very feeble*). Aye, soldier; just.

SOLDIER (*shouting up to the aspen top*). Good. I've come to take you home with me.

(*The Forest slowly recedes again.*)

WIFE. Husband! Husband! Why are you going to bed? The sun's still up and—

SOLDIER. I've got business to do.

WIFE. Business? In bed?

SOLDIER. That's what I said. Give me a kiss and go.

WIFE. Oh very well. Here's your kiss. I'll bring your supper in later.

(*The door closes.*)

SOLDIER. Supper? Ha! Ha! Now then, where's that nosebag? Patience, Death; I'm just about to unbuckle it.

DEATH (*muffled*). Thank you, soldier, thank you.

SOLDIER. But only on one condition.

DEATH (*muffled*). What's that?

SOLDIER. That, before you take anyone else, you take me.

DEATH (*muffled*). Why?

SOLDIER. I have had a sinful life and a long one. I reckon death will be best for me.

(*Pause.*)

Is that understood?

DEATH (*muffled*). Yes.

SOLDIER. Good. Then I'll let you out.

(*Musical Effect: the Nosebag Trick in reverse.*)

SOLDIER. Hey! Where are you off to?

DEATH. Catch me if you can.

SOLDIER. But you promised—

DEATH. I promised nothing. Do you think that I want to have any more truck with *you*?

SOLDIER (*pleadingly*). But Death, Death—

DEATH. It's no good begging my pardon. If people play tricks on me I can play tricks on them. You'll never see me again. Goodbye now and ill-luck to you.

(The door bangs.)

SOLDIER. Never see her again? That means I can never die. The beasts will die and the trees and everyone else but me. And I am a sinful man . . . sinful . . . sinful . . . . But there's an idea. They have a place for sin. I know what I'll do; I'll take me off to Hell. Just as I am. I'll pay for my sins alive. And I only hope it will be warm.

(A tocsin is heard in the far, far distance. It grows louder. Hell is in a state of alarm.)

DEVIL CAPTAIN. Sergeant!

4TH DEVIL. Sir?

DEVIL CAPTAIN. Who gave orders for that?

4TH DEVIL. For what, sir?

DEVIL CAPTAIN. For the tocsin.

4TH DEVIL. You did, sir.

DEVIL CAPTAIN. *I* did?

4TH DEVIL. Yes, sir. Two and twenty years ago. Remember, sir? The soldier with the nosebag.

DEVIL CAPTAIN. *That* fellow! You don't say *he* is—

4TH DEVIL. Yes, sir. He was seen at 00. hours approaching the West Gate. He ought to be there by now.

DEVIL CAPTAIN. The sentries got their instructions?

4TH DEVIL. Yes, sir. But if I was you, sir—

DEVIL CAPTAIN. You're quite right, Sergeant. I'll go along myself.

(The tocsin reaches a peak, then fades away.)

SOLDIER. But I tell you, devil, I'm guilty. I'm a guilty soul to be tortured.

SENTRY. Can't help that. You're alive.

SOLDIER. Alive? Maybe, but—

SENTRY. We don't take in no live 'uns. Besides, *you've* got a nosebag.

SOLDIER. What's that got to do with it?

SENTRY. It's a standing order of ours. Any soldiers with nosebags—

DEVIL CAPTAIN (*arriving*). What's the trouble here, sentry?

SENTRY. *He* is, Captain.

SOLDIER. Scaly! We meet again.

DEVIL CAPTAIN. Oh no, we don't. Get away there from the gates. Off with you into space. We've got no room for you here.

SOLDIER. But, Scaly, I've come to be tortured.

DEVIL CAPTAIN. Tortured? Ha! Ha! Ha! You'll be a lot more tortured drifting around in space. Rents are high in hell. Think that we'd let a practical joker like you—

SOLDIER. Any little corner—I'm not particular—

DEVIL CAPTAIN. You go away somewhere else. And in double quick time, do you hear?

SOLDIER. Somewhere else? Where?

DEVIL CAPTAIN. They say there's a place called Heaven—

SOLDIER. Heaven? They wouldn't look at me. Unless . . . unless . . . Scaly, do me a favour. And then I'll leave you in peace.

DEVIL CAPTAIN. What is it?

SOLDIER. Give me two hundred souls. Black ones out of the Pit. To take with me up to the gates of Paradise. Then perhaps they'll forgive me my sins and—

SENTRY. Well, of all the nerve!

DEVIL CAPTAIN. Shut up, sentry. Anything to get rid of him. Two hundred souls did you say. If you'll take yourself off at once—and promise not to come back—I'll throw in an extra fifty.

SOLDIER. That a deal?

DEVIL CAPTAIN. Two hundred and fifty souls from the Pit. Take 'em away and be blessed to you!

(*Ethereal music mounts with the souls through space.*)

ROBBER SOUL. Well, well, well, ain't it cool up here? Anyone got a spare sheepskin?

FEMALE SOUL. What I want to know is: how much higher are we going?

CROOK SOUL. Soldier, hey, soldier! The lady here—

ROBBER SOUL. Lady? Ha! Ha! Ha!

CROOK SOUL. The lady here would like to know where you're taking us.

SOLDIER. Why! Didn't the devils tell you? I'm taking you all to Paradise.

(*The Bad Souls murmur in astonishment.*)

ROBBER SOUL. Paradise!

FEMALE SOUL. Wings, you mean? And harps? What luck that I've kept my complexion.

ROBBER SOUL. Kept your complexion? Where?

(*The Bad Souls break into coarse laughter.*)

SOLDIER. Stop laughing, you fools. Look yonder.

CROOK SOUL. Hm! What's that? The sun's so bright in my eyes I can't exactly—

SOLDIER. The sun's below you, brother. That's the Gate.

THE SOULS. The Gate! . . . The Gate of Paradise!

SOLDIER. That it is, so you'd better behave decent.

CROOK SOUL. Decent? And why not? When in Rome, as I said when I cheated the Grand Tartar—But one point, soldier, do we have to pass through the Customs?

SOLDIER. Why do you ask that?

CROOK SOUL. Well, they're only trifles of course but as I was leaving Hell—

FEMALE SOUL. Look, darlings, look! I can see the pearly ramparts.

ROBBER SOUL. Yus, and I can see some fellows up there with spears. Watching us too, they are. Don't look too good to me.

(*A pause while we switch to Paradise.*)

OFFICER. Gatesman.

GATESMAN. Yes, sir.

OFFICER. What's that crowd down there? They on their way here?

GATESMAN. Yes, sir. Two hundred and fifty guilty souls from Hell and one live soldier with nosebag from—er—Earth.

OFFICER. Oh, indeed?

GATESMAN. What shall I do, sir? Give 'em the rightabout turn?

OFFICER. No. Let 'em come in. Two hundred and fifty's a nice round number.

GATESMAN. Two hundred and fifty-one, sir.

OFFICER. Two hundred and fifty I said. Can't have that soldier in here.

GATESMAN. Right, sir. I understand. They're coming up now, sir.

OFFICER. Good. Give the order to the Gates.

GATESMAN. Yes, sir.

(He turns and shouts out the formula.)

Gates!
Gates of Paradise!
Stand by to admit two hundred and fifty souls.
Gates! Unbolt! Swing on your hinges! Open!

(Music opens the gates.)

SOLDIER. Here, you.

ROBBER SOUL. Me?

SOLDIER. Quick. Take hold of this nosebag. As you go in, say to me—get this right—Say to me 'Soldier, jump into the nosebag'.

ROBBER SOUL. All right, all right, let go of it.

SOLDIER. But don't forget—this is my only chance—so don't forget, promise me, don't forget . . . .

(The Gatesman's voice rings out.)

GATESMAN. Gates!
Gates of Paradise!
Stand by to close!
Swing on your hinges. Close!

(Music closes the gates. Silence. The Soldier is alone.)

SOLDIER. So he forgot, the pig! And took my nosebag with him.

Well, that's the way things are. These gates will never open again for me. And Hell's out of it too and Death she won't come near me. Nothing for it, I reckon. Can't stay hanging round here; it's cold in space tonight. I can fancy a worse thing now than a place on a Russian stove and music maybe and a pipe of tobacco. I think I'll go back to earth.

(*A balalaika steals in; then peasant chatter. He has been here before.*)

MARYA. Landlord! Remember that soldier many years gone come in here once with three wild geese in a nosebag?

LANDLORD. The one that drove the devils out of the Tsar's palace?

MARYA. That's him, landlord. He's here again.

(*Incredulous exclamations all round.*)

LANDLORD. What! I heard he'd died.

SOLDIER (*himself again*). No, landlord; no such luck. Here's my last rouble; bring me some vodka.

LANDLORD. Marya, a bottle of vodka.

SOLDIER. Well, what's the news round here since I've been gone?

LANDLORD. News! Where've you been? The country's gone to war.

SOLDIER. War?

LANDLORD. Aye. They'll soon be calling on you.

SOLDIER. Not on me. I am a man of sin.

LANDLORD. Sin? Don't make me laugh. You're a soldier, ain't you?

SOLDIER. I was a soldier once. Then they discharged me.

LANDLORD. How much service did you have?

SOLDIER. Twenty-five years.

LANDLORD. Not much.

MARYA. The vodka, masters.

LANDLORD. Thank you. Fill up the soldier's double.

MARYA. He looks as if he can do with it.

SOLDIER. You're right, woman. Here's to—

LANDLORD. Not yet, soldier, not yet. *I'm* going to give you a toast. You've had twenty-five years of service? Well; you're going to have more. Campaigns like you never dreamed of. You had a magic nosebag, I see you've lost it. Well, that don't matter, you've got something better. You've got a—

SOLDIER. I've got a terrible thirst. Give me your toast.

LANDLORD. You've got a fighting heart and a fighting arm. Well, now you're going to fight with 'em. That's what you're going to do, all through the centuries, you are. Tartars, Swedes, French, Teutons—

SOLDIER. That will all come when it comes. Give me your toast.

LANDLORD. All right, soldier. Here's to Mother Russia.

SOLDIER. Here's . . . to Mother . . . Russia!

THE MARCH HARE SAGA

(1) *The March Hare Resigns*

(2) *Salute to All Fools*

TO

ESMÉ PERCY

INTRODUCTORY NOTE

The two March Hare programmes, written on the principle of a-little-bit-of-mud-for-everyone, both managed to outrage a large number of listeners. Partly because these listeners could not adjust themselves to what was happening (a *serial* crazy like *Itma* makes such an adjustment less drastic), partly because of their mistaken assumption that satire must be partisan, and partly because of their instinctive desire to pigeonhole everything—fun must be pure fun, satire must be pure satire, you can't be serious and frivolous simultaneously. Thus *The March Hare Resigns* made one listener complain that, *as a satire on planning*, it was pulling its punches (I leave it to the readers of the text to decide whether this listener's premise was correct). Still more surprisingly, *Salute to All Fools* provided the Social Credit Party with a sermon, based on a comparison of this programme with *Itma*: The *Itma* team 'feel with unthinking gusto. But you cannot THINK yourself into feeling with unthinking gusto'. Unthinking gusto, I must confess, is something I have never aimed at. And the Social Creditors' slogan of 'Feeling first'—whether or not it will solve, as they promise, the world's problems—has not normally been a guiding principle of writers of satirical fantasy. See Aristophanes.

The first object of both these programmes was, I must admit, entertainment. I am fond of nonsense literature. But even Lewis Carroll, in passing, throws light on his own times, gives a 'criticism of life'. I am publishing both these scripts because, though they often cover the same ground, and include indeed some of the same gags, they use a different emphasis. *The March Hare Resigns* is the more lyrical, its basic theme being the clash between the poetic (and sympathetic) madness of the Hare and the pedestrian (and repellent) madness of everyone else. *Salute to All Fools* rubs in much more salt; compare the Gael with the Smuggler, the Colonel with the Squire, the Marxist and the Scientist with the Planner and the Utopian. The latter, I think, was the better programme, not only because it has more bite but because the dialogue is crisper and the whole construction tighter; in *The March Hare Resigns* the characters are less significant and the transitions are often quite arbitrary.

Salute to All Fools was also better produced, as I made a point of getting speed in it; this was the easier thanks to the substitution of Nonesuch for Fitzpotter as second lead. As the March Hare must often fall into a grand and measured manner, the elementary radio principle of contrast requires that his feed should be quick; the Travelogue style, which Fitzpotter had to use, precluded this. In both programmes the March Hare goes on a tour; here Mr. Hopkins' music was invaluable. Any tour being an identity in difference, we used in each case a stock theme (*Over the Hills and Far Away* in the first programme and *Alleluia, I'm a Bum* in the second) which could be varied according to its context. Talking of identities in difference, I should add that the two broadcasts, though a year apart, were more closely related to each other (so forming what I have called a Saga) by the presence in both of Mr. Esmé Percy. Without him either of them might well have been a frost. I know of no other actor who could so convincingly and sympathetically be-hare himself. In the last minutes of *The March Hare Resigns* he achieved—what I wanted but what was almost too much to ask—a perfect transition from brittle fantasy to lyrical warmth. Both those who missed and those who resented this sudden intrusion of feeling I must class among the pigeon-holers. The fact that I think every institution and dogma—and nearly every person—need mocking has not made me a cynic.

CAST

The March Hare Resigns was first broadcast in the B.B.C. Home Service on March 29th, 1945. The main parts were played as follows:

THE MARCH HARE	ESMÉ PERCY
MINISTRY OFFICIAL	ALAN HOWLAND
FITZPOTTER	MACDONALD PARKE
YES-MAN	ARCHIE HARRADINE
DON	PETER USTINOV
HANSARD	BASIL JONES*
M.P.	ALEXANDER SARNER*
BUILDER	ROGER SNOWDON*
PLANNER	CYRIL GARDINER*
SQUIRE	BRYAN POWLEY*
MAGNATE	FRANK PARTINGTON*
MINER	BASIL JONES*
SMUGGLER	HARRY HUTCHINSON*
GENERAL DEBILITY	PETER USTINOV
LOVER	PETER NOBLE*
BELOVED	DOROTHY SMITH
THE FOUR LADIES	MOLLY RANKIN,* GRISELDA HERVEY,* ANN CODRINGTON,* MARJORIE WESTBURY*

Special music by Antony Hopkins.
The lyrics were sung by Archie Harradine.
Production by the author.

THE MARCH HARE RESIGNS

(*Musical Overture.*)

COMMENTATOR. The programme which follows was intended for All Fools' Day but, though it is not yet All Fools' Day, we hope this will find you as it leaves us. We present now: Salute to—

(*Crackling of script.*)

COMMENTATOR. I'm sorry—the wrong script; the right one has some mud on it. As this—er—precludes my reading the rest of the announcement, I leave you now in the paws of the March Hare.

(*Fanfare.*)

MARCH HARE. Ladies and gentlemen—Just a moment while I hang some daffodils over the microphone . . . There! What an exquisite pink. Now what was I saying? . . . Oh yes, ladies and gentlemen . . . But you aren't, you know; far from it. If you were you wouldn't be listening to *me*; you can't touch pitch, my dears. I got some pitch on my paws as I came up Portland Place. I was dancing as always—I have to dance by my nature—and having my eyes closed in a vernal ecstasy I bumped into a prefabricated non-existent bungalow. So the pitch was sticky of course—but I did a leg-glide and here I am in the studio. Hare Marches On! But not for ever, alas!

You've heard the terrible news? Parliament met today in secret session and they've decided that this year March is to end on the 31st—and be succeeded by April. So sudden, isn't it? And you see how that affects *me*? Being a March Hare I am a mad hare, but, *if* March comes to an end, why, then I lose my status; I become sane—like you; I cease to be myself! And what could be worse than that? Why, I'd rather be jugged.

WAITRESS'S VOICE. One jugged hare coming up! One jugged hare coming up!—Look out though; he'll bite.

HARE. Yes, of course I'll bite; I've bought a new denture at Christie's. But as I was saying—

There is a tide in the affairs of hares
Where March gives way to April. There's the rub:
To be or not be mad. Which not to be
Is not to be myself. And, not himself,
Why should the March Hare live?

A FLAT VOICE (*near*). Yes, why indeed?

HARE. It seems then I am doomed. Big Ben moves on;
The month of March which came in like a lion
Will go out like a lamb—mint-sauce and all—
And I shall then be sane. Could I but halt
The spiteful calendar—

AN IRISH VOICE. Why don't ye try? Ring up one o' them Ministries; they'll fix it for ye surely.

HARE (*matter-of-factly*). Thank you, my friend; that's a most unreasonable suggestion. I'll ring up the Ministry of . . . of . . .

A GOLDEN VOICE. Information?

HARE. No, no, no; they might give me some. I'll ring up the Ministry of Flops and Stoppages.

(*A telephone rings—orchestrally—till stopped by a Ministry Official, who, tired and hedging, speaks as if he had a cigarette in his mouth. In the pauses in the following speech the Hare is heard jibber-jabbering distortedly at the far end of the line.*)

MINISTRY OFFICIAL. Hullo? Hullo? . . . Yes, this is the Ministry of Flops and Stoppages . . . . Oh is that the March Hare? Well, what can we do for you, sir? . . . Have the calendar stopped, did you say? And the current month indefinitely extended? Well, I'm not quite sure that—
. . . Oh yes, we *do* but this is a biggish order. No precedent for it since *I've* been here. I'm afraid that in face of public opinion—what did you say? . . . An unknown quantity? You really think so? Well, in that case, if you could do a galloping survey or something—if you can discover a

quorum of persons throughout this country to agree to your scheme for the prolongation of March—well then, having weighed the evidence, we *might* see our way to— What's that? . . . You'd like to start on your galloping survey at once? . . . No, there's nothing against it but you realise of course that the Ministry can't at this stage commit itself—

(He falls back on false heartiness.)

Look, old boy—old hare, I mean—why not call around here before you start on your tour and we'll give you someone to cook it for you? Yes, yes, a kind of a guide. O.K., Hare, I'll expect you.

(The telephone clicks off.)

HARE. There! A ray of hope! Open that studio door—I'm off on my dancing survey!

A PUBLIC ADDRESS VOICE. Change here for Bedlam and Widdershins! Change here for Bedlam and Widdershins! First stop—Whitehall. Whitehall!

(Tour music.)

COMMISSIONAIRE. Sorry. You can't enter this building without a pass.

HARE. Oh! Can I enter with a somersault?

(A violent crash.)

MINISTRY OFFICIAL. Somebody's falling upstairs; that must be the March Hare.

HARE. It is! It is I myself! Now where is that impresario?

MINISTRY OFFICIAL. Impres—You mean the guide. I'm assigning you Mr. Fitzpotter here. He knows this country backwards—and forwards—*and* in technicolour.

FITZPOTTER. I sure do. Glad to meet you, Mr. Hare. I'll be delighted to conduct you round wonderful Britain, one of the most famous and unspoiled of all the North Sea Islands. Just come with me down this corridor.

(Tour music.)

HARE. Here I go—down the long corridors
Dancing and rollicking, chasing the impossible,
Drinking in the ozone, thinking the unspeakable
Until we come to—

(*The music stops.*)

FITZPOTTER. We come now to an old-world department in the Ministry of Flops and Stoppages, with its quaint colourless inhabitants—folk who from time immemorial—

(*He is interrupted by a moaning and wheezing in the background.*)

HARE. What's that, Mr. Fitzpotter?

FITZPOTTER. Some guy dying, I guess. Do you want a look-see?

(*A door opens. A pause.*)

FITZPOTTER. Yeah, he's dying all right. Do you want to ask him anything?

HARE. I do.

FITZPOTTER. Then make it snappy. The way he looks right now he—

HARE. My dying friend!

YES-MAN. Eh?

HARE. Would you consent to the year being stopped at March?

YES-MAN. Which year?

HARE. This year.

YES-MAN. *This* year! I haven't yet reached it. Last year's still priority. Isn't that so, Miss Stencil?

MISS STENCIL. Yes, Mr. Triplick. The files for 1945 are still in the decontamination room.

YES-MAN. I'm sorry, sir. Now go away and let me die. I've just been composing my owl-song.

MISS STENCIL. Swan-song, Mr. Triplick, swan-song.

YES-MAN. Quite so, Miss Stencil, owl-song.

(*He sings to the tune of The Tarpaulin Jacket:*)

A Ministry yes-man sat dying
At his desk in the midst of a mess;
When the Minister came to him sighing

He sighed back repeatedly: YES—
Yes, I must make another nice blue-print
(*Chorus*) blue-print
While my mood and my pencil are blue,
(*Chorus*) are blue
And I must write another white paper
(*Chorus*) papah
To prove we've done all we can do.
(*Chorus*) can do.

I know that I'm crossing the bar, sir—
I'll leave you my change of address—
But I trust that I shan't be too far, sir,
To cry through the stratosphere: YES—
Yes, I'll make you another nice blue-print
(*Chorus*) blue-print
I'll draft it up here in the blue—
(*Chorus*) the blue—
And I'll write you another white paper
(*Chorus*) papah
To prove we've done all we can do.
(*Chorus*) can do.

Now hear my last words as I'm dying:
Beware of Free Speech and the Press
And if anyone asks if you're trying
Be sure that you answer them YES—
Yes, we're making another nice blue-print—
(*Chorus*) blue-print—
Since the mood of the country is blue,
(*Chorus*) is blue,
And we're writing another white paper
(*Chorus*) papah
To prove we've done all we can do.

(*Chorus*) can do.

(*As the orchestra ends, a new voice enters the room—briskly.*)

DON (*approaching*). Miss Stencil! Regarding that memo—

MISS STENCIL. Hsh, sir. Look yonder.

DON. Dear me, dear me, another of my colleagues gone. And to look at him you wouldn't see the difference.

FITZPOTTER. You've said it, Prof. But to turn from the dead to the mad, have you met my friend the March Hare?

DON. Delighted! Delighted! So *you've* joined the Civil Service too? Then may I ask you a question—

HARE. May I ask *you* a question? I want to have the year stopped at March and—

DON. Stopped at March! You mean no more April?

HARE. No more April, no more May, no more June, no more—

DON. Yes, yes, I get your point. Personally, I'm opposed to it.

HARE. But—

DON. You see—this is off the record—in peace-time I'm a don. At All Fools' College, Oxford—you've heard of it of course? Our chef makes a very fine crème brûlé. Well, my work here in the Ministry's extremely interesting—interesting—but the truth of it is the pace is a bit too fast for me—fast. So, believe it or not, I'm looking forward to victory. And I can't have the year stopped in March because my friend old Moore—and *he* has very long ears—

HARE. So have I, so have I.

DON. So you have, sir, but please don't flick them at me. As I was saying, from my point of view, the year must move on and I must move back. Back to the Senior Common Room. And crème brûlé—brûlé!

FITZPOTTER. Come on, Hare. You haven't made first base yet. I know a place—a kind of a private house—where the residents like staying put.

HARE. They *like*—

FITZPOTTER. Yes, sir. Those old-timers, they've been sitting there now for nine and a half years, so I guess they must kind of enjoy it. So I propose we visit them. (*Slyly*) And we might find a couple of parties going on there.

HARE. Ah! Fun and games?

FITZPOTTER. Yes, sir. Musical chairs.

HARE. Come on. Let's go to this House!

(*Tour music.*)

FITZPOTTER. And so we come to happy Westminster with its dreaming towers and its innocent childish chatter—

HANSARD. Mr. Fitzpotter? Mr. M. Hare?

FITZPOTTER. That's right. How did you know?

HANSARD. I know everything. My name's Hansard. What can I do for you?

HARE. Find me a Member of Parliament—even one tiny back-bencher—to agree to the suspension of the calendar.

HANSARD. Suspension of the calendar? Hm. What you want is one of the members of the 1713 Committee.

FITZPOTTER. Why 1713?

HANSARD. Because Queen Anne wasn't dead then. Look! Here's one of them now. The honourable member for Oldways. Put him your question, Mr. Hare.

HARE. Sir, may I ask you—

M.P. I must have notice of this question.

HANSARD. It's about the reform of the calendar.

HARE. Yes, it's—

M.P. I would refer my honourable and furry friend to the statement made by Julius Caesar—

HARE. You mean *the* Julius Caesar?

M.P. Yes, sir, I'm a Preservative. When I once put my foot down—

HARE. Ow! . . . Ow!

M.P. I must ask you to withdraw that remark.

HARE. But you're standing on my paw, sir.

M.P. Possibly. In pursuance of Standing Order Number One—

One—One—One—One Mr. Speaker nominated me Chairman of Standing Committee XXXXX. It is therefore, sir, my duty to stand on people's paws.

HARE. Is it? Then take that, sir!

(*Sound of a slap.*)

HARE. In pursuance of Dancing Order Number 022-022-0 I nominate myself Chairman of Dancing Committee YYOY Not. And I hope that I'll dance on your grave, sir. Goodbye.

M.P. Unheard of! Unheard of!
Mr. Hansard, ask that hare why he doesn't carry a rear light.

HANSARD. I'm sorry, sir. He's adjourned, sir.

M.P. I'll be hanged.

HANSARD. Yes, sir. I'll be bound.

(*Tour music.*)

HARE. What have we here, Fitzpotter?

FITZPOTTER. Here we have one of the forgotten arts.

(*The orchestra drops bricks.*)

FITZPOTTER. An old-world builder dropping his bricks on the new world.

HARE (*calling up*). Builder! May I—

BUILDER. My name's Jerry. Heads below!

(*A single brick-drop.*)

HARE. Well now, Jerry, if you can spare the time—

BUILDER. I know what you want and I can't. I heard about you on the wireless and me answer's No, Mr. Hare. Get stuck in March! What next!

HARE. Nothing next.

BUILDER. Quite so! And what about all me prospects? See this here road? This is a wicked waste. Arterial road this is and it ain't got hardly no houses on it. Well, let me tell you this: once we gets victory over I reckon to line this here road with houses as far as Scotland. Look out, Guv'nor! Heads!

(*A brick drops.*)

HARE. My good man, is it part of your plan to brain your possible clients?

BUILDER. Plan! I ain't got no plan. I hates the sound of that word —and as for them nosey planners! (*He spits*) Why, there's a bloke up there—see where I'm pointing—that house on top of the hill what looks like it's made of glass—

(*A brick drops; Fitzpotter yells.*)

HARE. There, there, Fitzpotter; don't say it. Let's move on to the Planner's. People who live in glass houses won't, at least, drop bricks.

FITZPOTTER. No, but they'll drop suggestions. I don't like all this Brave New World stuff. I'd rather be in Tahiti.

HARE. Don't be so craven, Fitzpotter. Come! Let us mount the hill.

(*Brave New World music.*)

PLANNER. No, no, no, Mr. Hare, I'm afraid you are a reactionary. (*The Hare tries to protest.*) Have the year stopped! I won't have anything stopped. Perpetual progress, that's my watchword. Elsie, wind up the dialectic.

ELSIE. Yes, sir—and what about your beverage?

PLANNER. I'd like it hotter today—and while you're about it, Elsie, go to the refrigerator and bring me my model of the Future.

ELSIE. Yes, sir.

HARE. Why do you keep it in a refrigerator?

PLANNER. It walked in here with snow on its boots; if I keep it outside it goes bad. But that's our insular climate. As soon as I get the weather subjected to proper controls—it will need a big staff of course—

ELSIE (*returning, agitated*). Oh, sir! Oh sir!

PLANNER. What's wrong?

ELSIE. Those runner beans you planted—they're all turning into red tape.

PLANNER. Are they? Excellent. I'm very short of tape. You see, gentlemen, in the immediate future everyone—absolutely everyone—will be an employee of the State. Even you, Mr. Hare.

HARE (*alarmed*). Oh no, no, please not. The State and I—well, really, we're hardly on speaking terms. Ever since that day we oiled the watch with butter—it should have been margarine but—

PLANNER (*scandalised*). You oiled a watch with butter!

HARE. Yes. I did.

PLANNER. In that case . . . you must be liquidated. Elsie!

ELSIE. The rabbit-trap? Here, sir.

PLANNER. Right. You see this trap, Mr. Hare? For your own good I direct you now to walk into it. It is, as you see, stream-lined and air-conditioned—

(*A crash of breaking glass.*)

ELSIE. Oh sir! They've jumped right out through the wall. I told you that glass was breakable.

(*Tour music which segues into 'John Peel'.*)

SQUIRE. Upon my soul! If it isn't that lunatic hare! Well—and what've you been up to?

HARE. Dancin' and jumpin', Squire. But I've come to ask you a favour.

SQUIRE. Well, if you'd like a run with the beagles—

HARE. No, Squire, not today. This is a larger question. What lovely weather it is and how very well you're looking. You look very happy, Squire. Wouldn't you like to remain just as you are for ever?

SQUIRE. I *shall* remain just as I am for ever.

HARE. Oh well . . . what I really mean . . . .

SQUIRE. Come on! Come on!

HARE. Wouldn't you like this month to persist for ever? An eternity—an infinity—of March?

SQUIRE. March? Eternity? Don't talk rubbish. If there was only March in the year, think of what we should lose! April the

Second—Double Summer Time; Twelfth of August—grouse; First of September—partridge; First of October—pheasant—

HARE. But, Squire—

FITZPOTTER. It's no good, Hare. He certainly knows his mind.

SQUIRE. I should by now; I've had it for fifty years. You listen to me, my good animal. There may be chaps in the industrial cities who don't know one month from another, but—

HARE. May there? Come on, Fitzpotter!

(*Tour music.*)

FITZPOTTER. And so we come to the midmost parts of England, the workshop of Queen Victoria, home of forgotten exports and factory hooters, where the simple big-hearted magnates take care of their excess profits and, as if to remind us of—

MAGNATE (*Lancashire accent*). Come in, gentlemen. I understand you have a proposition.

FITZPOTTER. He has.

HARE. I have. I want the year stopped. Now!

MAGNATE. Eh? Then what about victory?

HARE. Victory?

MAGNATE. Aye. We shan't get victory this month, and, if we don't get victory, then we shan't have our boom, y'know.

HARE. What boom?

MAGNATE. What boom? Don't be daft. Haven't you heard of trade cycles?

HARE. No, I—I always keep off the roads.

MAGNATE. Eh? Look here; what's your profession?

HARE. Lunacy.

MAGNATE. Umph. Writer?

HARE. No, I—

MAGNATE. That's funny. Most lunatics *I* know are writers. Why do you wear that suit?

HARE. Suit? This is my skin!

MAGNATE. Utility fur, eh? Purchase tax on that. You don't belong to Common Health, do you?

HARE. Certainly not; I—

MAGNATE. Then you believe in private enterprise?

HARE. What's private enterprise, Fitzpotter?

FITZPOTTER (*unctuously*). It's a beautiful old world custom that—

MAGNATE. Excuse me, gentlemen, time's up. But remember what I said about the boom. Now then, where's my cycle?

(*Boom music; then workshop noises and workers' chatter.*)

HARE. So this is a factory. What is the odour?

FITZPOTTER. I don't know. Better ask the Drains Trust.

(*Through the tapping of hammers a Scots worker is singing slowly to the tune of 'Annie Laurie'.*)

1ST WORKER. 'There was a crooked man . . .'.

HARE. What's that man doing?

1ST WORKER. 'And he went a crooked mile . . .'.

FITZPOTTER. He's singing while he works.

1ST WORKER. 'He found a crooked contract . . .'.

HARE. Does that mean he's happy?

1ST WORKER. 'And he made a crooked pile—'
Happy? Ach! I'm doing overtime.

FITZPOTTER. He gets paid extra for that.

1ST WORKER. Aye and I've nothing to spend it on.

HARE. What about when the boom comes?

1ST WORKER. Och! What about when the slump comes? But it's all one to me. I'll be out of a job by then.

HARE. No more overtime?

1ST WORKER. No more any time. I'm just here because of the shortage of man-power. I'm unskilled, you see. They drafted me into this job. When peace comes back they'll throw me out on my ear.

HARE. And you won't like that?

1ST WORKER. Who says I won't like that? My heart's in the Highlands, my heart is not here, My heart's in the—

HARE. Which is your favourite month?

1ST WORKER. December.

HARE. Oh, not March?

1ST WORKER. Don't be foolish. Where does March get you?

HARE. Where does December get you?

1ST WORKER. It gets you to Hogmanay.

(*The workers laugh.*)

2ND WORKER (*Midland woman*). That's one for you, Mister.

HARE. Fitzpotter, this is desperate. I will speak to these people. Ladies and gentlemen—

(*Laughter and whistles.*)

FITZPOTTER. No, no, comrades.

HARE. Ladies and comrades, I have come to your factory with a simple proposal which will, I believe, confer great benefits on you all. All of you here have for five years or so enjoyed comparative security. You are so badly needed that nobody dares to sack you. But that may change, my friends. The time may come when you have to tighten your conveyor belts, to queue up once more at the doors of the Labour Exchanges and—if you are women—to be cooped up again in your homes—

2ND WORKER. I'd *like* to be cooped up in me home!

(*Cheers from the women.*)

HARE. Ladies and—

FITZPOTTER (*aside*). Comrades!

HARE. Comrades and comrades! The future is wrapped in clouds. 'Forty years on, getting colder and colder—'

3RD WORKER (*Northern girl*). Now laddie! No Jarrow school songs here, please!

HARE. I repeat; colder and colder. But here, in this factory, it's warm. And your present position is stable.

4TH WORKER. Stable? He's right! Like horses.

HARE. Please! You can clock in here each day that you want to—

5TH WORKER (*woman*). We don't want to clock in at all!

(*Cheers.*)

1ST WORKER. That's right. We want to go home.

4TH WORKER. We're sick of being transferred; we'd like to transfer ourselves.

(*Hear! Hear!*)

2ND WORKER. We've had our fill of E.W.O.; what we want is Tea for Two.

6TH WORKER. What we want is fags for fourpence.

4TH WORKER. What we want is beer that's beer.

1ST WORKER. And that's all still to come.

ALL. Hear! Hear!

HARE. It's no good, Fitzpotter. Take me somewhere else.

FITZPOTTER. Anywhere else?

HARE. Anywhere that you choose.

FITZPOTTER. O.K. I guess I know where that is.

(*A chord.*)

COMPÈRE. Hullo everyone. By special request we have pleasure in opening this afternoon's programme of Light Music with that popular number: 'Dream Soup'.

(*'Dream Soup' and chattering ladies.*)

1ST LADY (*gruff*). My dear, this band gets better every day. They're really almost good enough to broadcast.

2ND LADY (*cracked-sweet*). Yes, dear, they should—but then, the leader's profile—

1ST LADY. Wouldn't come out? I know!—but they say television's coming back soon.

2ND LADY. And those silly people in London lost my set in the Blitz! My dear! Just look who's come in. How unusual!

1ST LADY. You mean that hare?

2ND LADY. No, no, I mean the American.

(*'Dream Soup' continues to flow.*)

FITZPOTTER. And here we come, Mr. Hare, to an old-world five-star hotel, renowned for its cuisine and its distance from enemy action. The five stars are considered in popular lore to represent the following ancient British virtues: Self-Importance, Self-Repetition, Kindness to Pekes, Unearned Increment, and Indigestion.

(*'Dream Soup' ends; desultory clapping.*)

HARE (*aside to Fitzpotter*). Perhaps, now the band's stopped—shall I make my plea now?

FITZPOTTER. O.K. Go ahead. Shoot.

HARE. Comrades—

(*Gasps of indignation.*)

FITZPOTTER. Hsh!

1ST LADY. Who is this impertinent animal?

FITZPOTTER. Make it more formal, you sap.

HARE. Ladies of England, pillars and columns of society, I come before you today with a sword hanging over my head—

2ND LADY. *I* don't see any sword.

1ST LADY. It's a metaphorical sword, dear.

HARE. It's not, it's an infra-red sword. And that being so, I must beg you—

WAITER. Sorry, sir; no begging allowed in here.

HARE. Oh very well, I'll demand. Here and now in the name of the Hounds of Spring—of whom I'm the M.F.H.—

1ST LADY. Oh so he hunts; that's different.

HARE. In the name of the flowers of this month—forsythia and almond, oxlip and coaltip, crocus and pocus, in the name of the Emergency Flowers Act itself, in the name of your own antecedents—your altruistic activities, your welfare work in the County, your endless successes at bridge—

3RD LADY (*hard and high*). Don't flatter us, my dear beast. We did lose that rubber in Malaya.

(*Hsh! Hsh!*)

HARE. Oh let foregones be foregones. In the name of—

1ST LADY. In the name of goodness what are you driving at, sir?

HARE. I want to stop the calendar.

LADIES. To what?

HARE. I wish the year to stay where it is and never move forward again.

(*The ladies gasp.*)

3RD LADY. Never . . . move . . . ? . . . !

HARE. Does anyone here second me?

1ST LADY. Second you! It's my belief, sir, you're mad. Stop the year where it is!

(*The band strikes up a 'Continental' theme.*)

1ST LADY. When we've just made our plans for the summer!

LADIES. So have we all! So have we all!

4TH LADY (*bubbling*). You see, Mr. Hare, as soon as this war's over, we're going to revisit the Continent.

On the road to Biarritz
Which no debutante omits
And the dawn comes up like Pernod—and you might be in the Ritz.

1ST LADY.

On the road to Ancient Rome
Underneath Bramante's dome
And the dawn comes up like Verdi and it's such a home from home.

3RD LADY.

On the road to the Tyrol
Where one feels one has a soul
And the dawn is wunderschoener and the hats are—oh, so droll.

2ND LADY.

On the road to Bukarest
Where the men were all well-dressed
And the dawn came up too early and—er—perhaps you know the rest.

1ST LADY. On the road to Carcassome—

HARE. Well, I really must be gone.

When you land in Europe wire me (*he turns away*)—tell me

how you're getting on.

(*The door bangs; the band and the Safe Hotel recede.*)

FITZPOTTER. Hey there, Hare! Don't go so fast. Watch your step now.

HARE. I must get out, I must get out, I must get out.

FITZPOTTER. Well, that's the umbrella stand on your right—and that's a bed of pinks on your left—and right there in front of you, that's the lily pond.

UTOPIAN (*very slow*). If you want to reach Utopia, walk on the dotted line.

HARE. And who are you, sir?

UTOPIAN (*slower still*). I am a man whose ideas outpace the clock.

HARE. And the calendar?

UTOPIAN. *And* the calendar.

HARE. Oh!

UTOPIAN. I am a Front Room Boy. Things can't ever move fast enough for me. You come into my lab and I'll show you what I'm working on. Know what it is? The Mill . . . enn . . . i . . . um!

Yes, *I* know where I'm going.

(*splash as he falls into the water.*)

FITZPOTTER. And so we leave our long-sighted friend in the lily pond, and, turning our backs upon Safe Hotels and Utopias, we go on our way once more, passing a mobile canteen—

HARE. Don't let's pass. I'm hungry.

CANTEEN WAITRESS. Hungry, Mister? Here you are.

(*A plate is slapped down on a counter.*)

CANTEEN WAITRESS. Cut off the joint and two veg.

HARE. Ah, two veg! But where's the—er—

CANTEEN WAITRESS. Cut off the ration? You've had it.

(*A plate is snapped away again.*)

FITZPOTTER. And so we go on our way, leaving a cold plate and looking for a warm answer. But who will give us this answer?

HARE (*with sudden intuition*). I know! The Average Man.

FITZPOTTER (*slyly*). Yeah—and the Average Woman.

(*Tour music.*)

HARE. Are you the Average Man?

MEN (*in unison*). We are the Average Man.

HARE. Are you the Average Woman?

WOMEN (*in unison*). We are the Average Girl.

HARE. Then—to begin with the ladies—You, madam, are *not*, I take it, planning to spend your summer upon the Continent?

(*The answer is given by a chain of voices.*)

WOMEN. Nay lad don't talk daft what do 'ee think us is dinna ye ken ye fule we ain't got no time for the Continent.

(*All together.*) Not *this* summer! No!

HARE. Excellent. Now you, sir? You aren't, I assume, banking on any Utopia?

MEN. 'OO? Me! Banking! Blimey! That's proper nonsense y'know ee if you was to ask me lad if you ask me chum ye'd steer clear of Utopias *and* myopias *and* cornucopias—and keep your money in a tea-pot.

(*All together.*) Utopias for *us*? No!

HARE. Fitzpotter! At last! Here are two types at least who are after my own heart. This couple want to stay put.

MEN AND WOMEN. Eh! Just a moment!

Stay . . . put . . . *where*?

HARE. In the month of March. For ever!

GIRL. Oh no you don't.

WOMEN. No you don't!

HARE. But why, if—

GIRL. Stay put in March! With the Spring Fashions to come! And me that's saved me coupons!

WOMEN. That's right.

HARE. Then I turn to you, sir. Will you, as a man of reason—

MEN. Stay put in March? No!

1ST MAN. Miss our Easter Monday!

The March Hare Resigns

WOMAN. We may not want summer on the Continent—

2ND MAN. But we do want our next Bank Holiday—

(They all cheer and set the mood for a lyric.)

TENOR. Easter Monday's just around the cor-ner,
I'm orf to find the World that Never Was,
I missed the bus before but I feel no longer sore
For I'm going to make the grade today because . . .
I 'opes to take a nip in The Case is Al-tered,
I 'opes to play me fiddle while Robbie burns,
And then look in on the Goat and the Tote and the Eagle
And *then* I'll sink a pint in The Dog Returns.

CHORUS. Oh the Bank
Holiday, holiday, holiday!
The Bank
Holiday, holiday, hic!
The Bank
Holiday, holiday, holiday!
The Bank, Bank
Holiday, holiday hic!

TENOR. The only Girl in the World is on the car-pet,
We're orf to 'ave a spree as never was;
She slapped my face before but it feels no longer sore
And today she'll be quite diff-e-rent because . . .
We're orf to 'it it 'igh in The Case is Al-tered—
We're orf to spend a spot of what we earns—
We're orf to drink in the Bell and the Smell and the Benbow
And one for the road in The Dog Returns.

CHORUS. Oh the Bank
Holiday, holiday, holiday!
The Bank
Holiday, holiday, hic!
The Bank
Holiday, holiday, holiday!

The Bank, Bank
Holiday, holiday, hic!

(*As the orchestra ends, a cheer-leader gives three cheers—Hic! Hic! Hooray!*)

HARE. The dog returns—but *I* move on. Oh this England! Let's try Wales.

(*Tour music—turning Welsh.*)

FITZPOTTER. And so we come to the picturesque old mining village of Cymric-ap-pliss-don't-come-agen.

MINER. That is not the way to pronounce it.

HARE. Excuse me. Are you a Bevin Boy?

MINER. I am not. I am a professional.

HARE. Would you like the calendar stopped?

MINER. I would not. If the calendar is stopped my wages is stopped. Besides the war will end soon and then we may open new seams. In a new pit, you know. In my present pit the coal-face runs away from me.

HARE. I sympathise. My face does that too. If I weren't so quick with my paws it would soar up—oh, so high—

MINER. How high? Top C?

FITZPOTTER. No, his face is a bass.
Gosh, it's beginning to rain.

MINER. Yes, how wet is my business.

HARE. Rain? Rain? What can we do about this?

MINER. Will you come down in the mine?

HARE. No, no, no; we'll go to Ireland.

(*Tour music—turning Irish.*)

HARE. My friend! You've dropped a parcel. Just over there on the Border.

SMUGGLER. Thank ye, sir. I know I have.

HARE. But why—

SMUGGLER. Whisht! I'm a smuggler.

FITZPOTTER (*beginning to gush*). Ah! The historic custom of smuggling—

SMUGGLER. Yes, but it's fallin' off, sir. That's why I'm lookin' forward now to the summer.

HARE. So *you're* looking forward too?

SMUGGLER. Indeed I am. I'm expectin' a General Election. It's as certain as grass is green and lilies is orange. I'm afraid I've missed the Dail but Stormont will do just as well.

FITZPOTTER. Gee! You don't mean that *you*—

SMUGGLER. I mean that I want a seat. I'm sick an' tired of clamberin' over these fences; I want somewhere to park meself. They tell me that houses of Parliament always has easy chairs.

HARE. But do you think you'll get in?

SMUGGLER. Get in, is it? Haven't I took a large-sized herd of cattle and—

(He is cut off by an angry shout.)

GENERAL. Contact! Contact!

SMUGGLER. Look out. That'll be the general. Mind the air-screw now. He's just takin' off for England.

HARE. Then perhaps he'll give us a lift. What is his name?

SMUGGLER. Ach, I wouldn't know. He's a fine old English gentleman.

(The General's fanfare.)

FITZPOTTER. Beg pardon, General; could we bum a ride on your airplane?

GENERAL. What's that, sir? I'm deaf.

HARE. We hope you won't deem us cavalier but—

GENERAL. No good that rabbit talking. I never could hear what they say.

HARE. Rabbit! May I inform you I'm not a—

GENERAL. Not in the habit? Quite so. Cooked but not heard's the motto.
Come on there! Contact! Contact!
Where are those blank effects? Where's that gramophone girl?

GRAMS GIRL (*cooingly*). I'm sorry, General. The censor sat on the disc.

GENERAL. Oh all right; take it as played . . . .

(*Pause.*)

Gentlemen, we are now air-borne.

FITZPOTTER. Then I guess we'd better introduce ourselves. My name is—

GENERAL. My name is General er—General er—Dammit, I've forgotten again . . . My name is General Debility.

FITZPOTTER. My name is—

GENERAL. You look to me like a journalist. Tell me: has Mafeking been relieved yet?

FITZPOTTER. Yes, sir.

GENERAL. Good. I had a bet with a fellow—he was a bit of a bore —that before I died—That's what I'm up to now, you know.

HARE. What, sir?

GENERAL. Dying. I die on the First of April.

HARE. But why on the—

GENERAL. Can't die in March. Too cold.

HARE. Well, in *that* case—As long as March remains, *you* must remain. So if you don't want to die—

GENERAL. Who said I don't want to die?

Effects there! Effects!. . . All right; take 'em as played. Very nice landing that. And here, all ready to meet us, is my great friend, Major er—Major er . . . .

(*The Major's fanfare.*)

GENERAL. Ah yes, my friend Major Drawback. Anything you want to know; just ask him and he'll sink it.

MAJOR. What *do* you want to know, gentlemen?

HARE. We want to know if you'd agree—

MAJOR. I never agree to anything. Next question. Don't keep me waiting.

HARE. Well, regarding the months of the year, what do you think—

MAJOR. I never think.

HARE. Well, um, well . . . in that case . . . .

MAJOR. When you've any more to say, if you have, you'll find me over there in the club-house. Good day to you, gentlemen.

HARE. Oh dear! . . . Shall we follow him?

FITZPOTTER. Shall we follow him! Come, Hare; walk with me in the steps—size twelve—of an old English major and while on our way to the club-house—

(*His attention is distracted by the murmur of two voices. At the same time the orchestra has crept in with a love-theme.*)

FITZPOTTER. What have we here on the fairway?

(*The Hare and the listeners eavesdrop.*)

HARE. 'In the spring a leveret's fancy—' I don't think we should disturb them.

(*The music ends and the young couple turn towards him.*)

LOVER (*slightly cockney*). You can't disturb us. We're happy!

BELOVED (*Scots*). We're so happy we want to share it with everyone.

LOVER. Yes, because, you see, we'll never be so happy again.

HARE. What's that?

BELOVED. Och, what Jim means is it'll be sort of different.

HARE. Then in *that* case—

BELOVED. And the weather's so lovely now. I think this is just the loveliest time of the year.

HARE. Then listen to me; I—

BELOVED. Of course we do look forward to getting married.

LOVER. Yes, we've seen just the house we want but somebody else has got it.

BELOVED. Besides, we couldn't afford it—not when the war's over. I'll be out of my job and Jim, poor lamb, he'll be—

HARE. But, my dear children! You're just the people I've been looking for. You say you couldn't be happier than you are at this moment?

BELOVED. That's right.

HARE. And you say your future is doubtful?

LOVER. That's right.

HARE. Then why not stop the clock—nay, stop the calendar? Stay for ever here in the fairway of the Present. In the kindly winds of March which flutter the flags on the greens and—

LOVER. Oh we couldn't do that. (*With a blush in his voice.*) The wedding's in June.

HARE. But you may not have anything to live on.

BELOVED. That's right. Still we do want a house of our own and—

HARE. Endless housework, bills choking the letter-box, tea-leaves choking the sink—Goodbye to the neiges d'antan, the perquisites of passion. And then middle age. And old age.

BELOVED. Och, that's a long way off. Jim and I—we're young still.

HARE. Yes. You're *terribly* young.

(*Pause.*)

Come, Fitzpotter. I give up. Nobody cares about March, nobody cares for the poor March Hare, nobody wants to stay put. The calendar must go on—three hundred and sixty-five days and all the routine as usual. I'm returning to base. Back to that studio in Broadcasting House. My positively last appearance. For after this I resign.

And you—you two children—goodbye. I hope you'll never regret . . . what was a very good offer.

(*Tour music—slow. When it ends he is back in the studio.*)

HARE. Ladies and gentlemen, I return to this microphone defeated. I have toured your country without finding any support. You have let down your March Hare. It seems that madness—of my kind—is vieux jeu. And March is now running out—like precious sugar from a leaking bag. There is little more sweetness left. The day after the day after tomorrow I shall be no longer myself. As a common hare I shall feel uncommonly dull. But you—what do you care?

The March Hare Resigns

Pursuing the course of your sanity, you will stand in queues as ever, fighting for places on elevators and escalators, on band-wagons and non-stop wagons-lits. But let me not be ungenerous. The moment my doom is sounded and March turns into April, I wish you all many happy returns of the day—and on April the First may you all fool each other. I shall be fooled no more. A winged shadow is coming up from the South. It is the first cuckoo. 'In April come he will.' Summer is i-cumen in—Hare he is a-dancin' out. For I cannot go down fighting but I shall go out dancing. I snap my fingers at you and your stupid calendar. And here and now—you've been waiting for this—I resign!

(*A cuckoo calls; then musical finale: 'Summer Is I-Cummen In'.*)

CAST

Salute to All Fools was first broadcast in the B.B.C. Home Service on April 1st, 1946. The main parts were played as follows:

THE MARCH HARE	ESMÉ PERCY
NONESUCH	HOWARD MARION-CRAWFORD
LITTLE BIT OF PAPER	MARJORIE WESTBURY★
PHOTOGRAPHER	STANLEY GROOME★
JOE	TOMMY DUGGAN
THE JOURNALISTS' TRUTH	GWEN DAY BURROUGHS
POET	BASIL JONES★
POETIC TRUTH	CHERRY COTTRELL
NEO-YOGI	LAIDMAN BROWNE★
COLONEL	CYRIL GARDINER★
TORY TRUTH	GLADYS YOUNG★
MARXIST	CHARLES LENO★
PSYCHO-ANALYST	RUDOLPH OFFENBACH
GAEL	HARRY HUTCHINSON★
SCIENTIST	RICHARD GOOLDEN

Special music by Antony Hopkins.

The lyrics were sung by Martin Boddy and Marjorie Westbury.

Production by the author.

SALUTE TO ALL FOOLS

ANNOUNCER. Salute to All Fools! No one has asked for this programme but here it is. Our subject tonight is Truth. Today being April the First, we consider this theme appropriate. Listeners will have the privilege of hearing a number of experts on Truth, all of them equally infallible; our question-master is the March Hare. For those who are still switched on, we now present:

Salute to—Salute to—Salute to—Salute to—etc. . . .

1ST VOICE (*rough*). Come on, come on, come on; get unstuck.

ANNOUNCER. Salute to—Salute to—Salute to—

2ND VOICE (*high and sweet*). All fools?

ANNOUNCER. Yes.

(*The programme proper now starts with a lyric to the tune of 'Alleluia, I'm a Bum'.*)

TENOR. Oh April the First
Is the feast of All Fools
Without any chairman,
Without any rules—
Howpeculiah! You're a fool,
Howpeculiah! Don't be sore.
Howpeculiah—begging your pardon
We must fool you once more.
(*The chorus repeats these four lines.*)

TENOR. No doubt you all think
You are perfectly sane
But on A-per-il Fool's Day
You'd best think again . . . .
(*A figure on the trumpet.*)

TENOR. Now salute to you all
From the depth of my heart;

CHORUS. If you'll keep on that wireless,
We're ready to start!

(*The orchestra stops. A 'common' voice steps patly into the silence.*)

NONESUCH. No, no, ducky. 'If the hat fits', my father used to say—

MOLLY. Yes, dear—but he was a hatter.

NONESUCH (*snobbishly*). One of the Mad Hatters, Molly. But his never did of course. The first fit he had, he died.

MOLLY. So that's why you gave up the business?

NONESUCH. That's it, ducky; wanted to better myself. Selling ideas? Yes. Selling passes? Yes. Selling pups? Yes. But selling hats? No!

MOLLY. And today you've become an Agent! But, Nonesuch dear, what are you an agent for?

NONESUCH. Oh um.... Theatre, television, test-matches, tiger-shooting—Everything that starts with T.

MOLLY. T?

NONESUCH. Yes, Molly; no black market—one-and-six the packet. (*He reels off the items at breakneck speed.*) Trumpet-players, trombone-players, trout-fishing; tennis-royal, tennis-table, tennis-lawn; tattoos-military, tattoos on the chest or back; taffeta, theology, thaumaturgy, titbits. Tossing the pancake, throwing the weight. Tin-mining, typing, terrorisation. And a few less important side-lines—things, you know, of one syllable: tips, tops, tiles, tubs, toques, tykes, times, tides, tar, tripe, tosh, trash—and, er, truth, of course.

MOLLY, Truth, Nonesuch?

NONESUCH. That's what I'm seeing this client about today. I wish it was something else. An old friend of my father's too. The March Hare. If he'd only come to me yesterday!

MOLLY. Why?

NONESUCH. Because it was March then. Then I could have sold him anything. But today—well, you see, he's not quite himself today and he's got this thing about truth.

MOLLY. The March Hare? Really?

NONESUCH. Yes, dear. Not what he used to be.

(*The chorus comes bang in:*)

The Old March Hare he ain't what he used to be,
ain't what he used to be, ain't what he used to be,
The Old March Hare he ain't what he used to be
only a day ago!
Only a day ago . . .etc.

(*The March Hare appears as the music ends.*)

MOLLY. Look, Nonesuch dear! What perfectly charming ears.

HARE. Ladies and gentlemen,—

VOICES. Hsh! The March Hare!

HARE. Ladies and gentlemen, you are quite right. A day ago I was officially mad. Throughout the month of March I was bound by the rules of my office to devote myself to fantasy. But today is the First of April, I am free to do what I like. The hares of Spring are on Winter's traces. I have decided to get married.

THE WOMEN. Married!

HARE. Yes, ladies, but not to you. The bride of my choice is Truth.

AN INCREDULOUS VOICE. Who?

HARE. Truth, I said. Today is the First of April. And that's why I've called on you, Mr. Nonesuch.

NONESUCH. At your service, Mr. Hare. Would you like her brunette or blonde?

HARE. Mr. Nonesuch! I am surprised at you. There is only one Truth in this world. You are my agent. Find her.

NONESUCH. Find her? Half a tick—Where did I put that address book?

(*A tiny voice pipes up.*)

LITTLE BIT OF PAPER. You don't need an address book.

NONESUCH AND HARE. Who's that?

LITTLE BIT OF PAPER. Only a little bit of paper.

NONESUCH. Only a—Where *are* you?

LITTLE BIT OF PAPER (*very fast, in Yellow Dog Dingo rhythm*). Here am I, just a little bit of paper, lying in the bottom of the waste-paper basket—very poor company down in this basket —yesterday's newspapers, all unread—last year's bills, all unpaid—tomorrow's blueprints—

HARE. All very blue?

LITTLE BIT OF PAPER. No, sir; all very pink.
But if you would be so kind as to read me—

HARE. Read you? With pleasure. Hand me that basket, Nonesuch. Now! Away you bills, you tram-tickets, you trash—Ah, my little friend, how ragged, how crumpled you are—

LITTLE BIT OF PAPER. Read me, Mr. Hare, read me.

HARE. Why, she's just an address.

LITTLE BIT OF PAPER. The Focus-Pocus studios, a Likeness while you Wait; photographers ex cathedra, par excellence, and in excelsis—

NONESUCH. That's it. It was on the tip of my tongue. Taxi! Taxi! You'll see the Truth in a tick, sir.

PHOTOGRAPHER. Tick!
There you are, Mr. Hare. The Truth, the whole Truth and nothing but the Truth. Developed, printed and mounted—and only five guineas per copy.

HARE. The whole Truth? But this is a picture of me! And not, I may say, a good one.

PHOTOGRAPHER. Why not, Mr. Hare?

HARE. Well, for one thing, my fur. It looks so . . . so . . . so moth-eaten.

PHOTOGRAPHER. Your fur *is* moth-eaten. That is the truth, Mr. Hare.

HARE. And one of my ears looks longer than the other.

PHOTOGRAPHER. One of your ears *is* longer than the other. That is the—

HARE. No, it is not! Come, Nonesuch. Truth is not here; the camera always lies.

PHOTOGRAPHER. Now look, Mr. Hare, I could touch you up, you know—

HARE. Touch me up!
What is our next address?

LITTLE BIT OF PAPER. Follow *me*! Follow *me*!

HARE. What's that? The voice of an oracle?

LITTLE BIT OF PAPER. No, no, no, just a little bit of paper blown by the wind through the gutters of London;

(*The Alleluia theme on the orchestra gets them moving.*)

LITTLE BIT OF PAPER. All who are anxious to find the truth must follow me, follow me, follow me quickly, for I am on my way to the home of Truth—through Piccadilly Circus, don't look round—past the National Gallery, don't go in—and along the Strand—

HARE AND NONESUCH. Along the Strand—

LITTLE BIT OF PAPER. And here we are—in Fleet Street!

(*The music ends. Here they are.*)

JOE (*pseudo-American*). Will you look who's here! Nonesuch, old boy!

NONESUCH. Joe! Joe, meet my friend the March Hare. Joe, here's an ace newspaper man.

JOE. Pleased to meet you, Mr. Hare. Fag-end? What can I do for you?

HARE. Introduce me to Truth.

JOE. Sure. Come right up to my office.

HARE. The lady is in your office?

JOE. Not if she's a lady.

HARE. Oh but—

JOE. That's O.K. Lady, did you say?

HARE. Of course Truth is a lady.

JOE. Does she dance?

HARE. Of course she dances.

JOE. O.K. Follow me, boys. Taxi there! Taxi!

NONESUCH. Where are you taking us, Joe?

JOE. Where do you think? The Charity Ball.

NONESUCH. The Char—

JOE. Bit of a zoo, I'm afraid. Driver, the Charity Ball.

HARE (*to himself, puzzled*). Bit of a zoo . . . a zoo? . . .

(*A kookaburra introduces other zoo voices which merge into a waltz and the chatter of human beings.*)

JOE. There she is now, old leveret. The one and only Truth, sir.

NONESUCH. Yes . . . the half-naked Truth. Nice bit of make-up though.

JOE. Sure. She knows her stuff. The one and only Truth—the Queen of Fleet Street.

JOURNALISTS' TRUTH. Talking about me, Joe?

(*Hsh! Hsh!*)

JOE. Yeah. Why not? I got you your entrée here.

JOURNALISTS' TRUTH. Lay off, brother. You Fleet Street boys seem to think you discovered me. Who's that animal with you?

JOE. Old Pussyfoot? He's your next boy-friend.

JOURNALISTS' TRUTH. Gee, another! Where's his credentials?

HARE. These are my credentials, madam. I am the March Hare and this is the First of April. I come of a noble, not to say nimble, family; my father won the high jump at the Olympic Games—my uncle won the boat-race—and in Ancient India an ancestor of mine was ambassador of the Moon. I can run in a circle, sleep with my eyes open, sing arias to the dawn and mend watches with butter. But now I search for Truth and if you, Madam, are she—

JOURNALISTS' TRUTH. Am I her! Say, Mr. Hare, if I wasn't a real lady, I would resent that. Am I Truth! Why don't you keep those long ears of yours to the ground?

HARE. Like this?

JOURNALISTS' TRUTH. Yeah. Like that. Now, brother, what do you hear?

HARE. I hear a million typewriters tapping out your praises, a hundred thousand rollers printing you new dresses—

NONESUCH. A new dress every day?

JOURNALISTS' TRUTH. A new dress every hour.

NONESUCH. Excuse me.

JOURNALISTS' TRUTH. You're welcome.

HARE. She *is* Truth, Nonesuch! She must be. Look at that mouth. The perfect Cupid's bow. Such a mouth could never tell a lie.

NONESUCH. 'Father, I cannot tell a lie. I did it with my little lipstick.'

HARE. She did not!

JOURNALISTS' TRUTH. I certainly did. You don't catch me leaving it all to Nature. Come on, big beast, why don't you ask me to dance?

HARE. But of course! When Truth and the March Hare meet what could be more to the point? To dance round cheek to cheek while the waltz goes on for ever—

(*The waltz ends.*)

HARE (*appalled*). Oh!

JOURNALISTS' TRUTH. That's too bad. Pardon me while I change my eyebrows.

POET. Leave your eyebrows alone! (*The crowd reacts.*) Madam, you are an impostress. I accuse you of false identity.

(*Exclamations.*)

JOURNALISTS' TRUTH. Really, young man? Who *are* you?

POET. I am a poet. Who are *you*?

JOURNALISTS' TRUTH. The name, brother, is Truth.

POET. Truth! *I* came here with Truth. She is my partner—from now till the end of the world.

JOURNALISTS' TRUTH. Is she? How come you weren't dancing?

POET. We have been sitting in the corner. That is she with her back to us.

NONESUCH. Pickled? Or just in a trance?

POET. In a trance, you common man. She is always entranced—and entrancing. Look, she is turning round.

POETIC TRUTH. I . . . am Truth.

(*This new and unreal voice sets the crowd whispering.*)

HARE. Was this the face that launched a thousand odes?

JOURNALISTS' TRUTH. If it was, it could do with some make-up.

POETIC TRUTH. Make way for me. I am Truth.

HARE (*aside*). Nonesuch, they can't both be!

NONESUCH. Hsh!

POETIC TRUTH. I am Truth, the partner of all poets.

JOURNALISTS' TRUTH. Then why don't you take the floor?

POETIC TRUTH. Because I take the sky. I beat in the void my ceaseless wings in vain. And only those can escort me who are also winged. Those who have inspiration.

POET. Which lets you all out but me.

HARE. Nonsense, sir. *I* have inspiration.

POETIC TRUTH. And who are *you*?

HARE. I am the March Hare.

POETIC TRUTH. Mad?

HARE. Yes.

POETIC TRUTH. Good.
In love with me?

HARE. Yes.

POETIC TRUTH. Better.
But do you know the answers?
What is a poet?

HARE. A poet is the unacknowledged legislator of the world.

POETIC TRUTH. How does he legislate?

HARE. By sitting in a corner. And burning always with a hard gem-like flame.

POETIC TRUTH. What use is this legislation?

HARE. No use at all.

POETIC TRUTH. Full marks.
What am I?

HARE. You are the plain Truth.

JOURNALISTS' TRUTH. Plain is the operative word.

POETIC TRUTH. Madam!

JOURNALISTS' TRUTH. Madam yourself, wall-flower!

(*Poetic Truth screams, Journalists' Truth jeers; the onlookers join in with gusto.*)

NONESUCH. Now, now, now, girls; let me introduce you. Miss . . . er . . . Truth—Miss . . . er . . . Truth.

JOURNALISTS' TRUTH. Truth! Take that.

(*A slap.*)

POETIC TRUTH. Truth! Take this.

(*Another slap.*)

NONESUCH. Look out! The police!

POLICEMAN. Here, here, here; identity cards, please. You first, madam.

(*Journalists' Truth groans.*)

HARE (*anxiously*). Is her name Truth?

POLICEMAN. No.

(*The crowd laughs.*)

POLICEMAN. And you, Madam?

(*Poetic Truth sighs.*)

HARE (*more anxiously*). Is *her* name Truth?

POLICEMAN. 'Course not.

(*The crowd laughs louder.*)

POLICEMAN. And you, sir, why are you flattening your ears?

HARE. Because I'm frightened, officer.

POLICEMAN. Frightened, eh? Then you'd better be off home. Where do you live?

HARE. I live in a form.

POLICEMAN. In form? You mean in order?

HARE. No, not in order at all. It's made of bracken, you see, and the housemaid left last week—

POLICEMAN. I see, I see. Well, you'd better go back and fill it in. But not in pencil, mind.

HARE. Of course not, I always use earth.

POLICEMAN. The *good* earth?

HARE. Yes, the good earth. That's where I live.

POLICEMAN. Then off with you there at once. You can get a bus outside.

HARE. Bus? Far be it from me. I'll take the Joyful Plough. Ahoy there, Joyful Plough! Wait for us, we're coming.

(*A rustic piece on the orchestra takes him and Nonesuch to the country.*)

HARE. So here we are, back to the Good Earth. But oh, Nonesuch, look at the mud on my paws.

NONESUCH. Well, mud's better than paw-cuffs. That couple of females all but got us in jug.

HARE. One of my uncles was jugged once. He never came back. But where is my own little form? It's not such a very good form but—

COLONEL. Not good form at all, sir. Breaking my fence like that!

HARE. Oh excuse me, Colonel; I didn't see you.

NONESUCH. And we didn't know it was your fence.

COLONEL. Didn't you? Couldn't you see me sitting on top of it? I've a good mind to summons you both for poaching.

HARE. Oh but we weren't. I never have anything to do with poachers. One of my uncles—

NONESUCH. We're just here in search of Truth, sir.

COLONEL. Oh, Truth? That's quite another matter.

(*He turns away and shouts.*)

Truth! Come here, my dear lady.

TORY TRUTH. (*shouting back gruffly*). What is it, Colonel?

COLONEL. She's deaf—poor old dear. Tory old age, you know. Come here, Truth! These gentlemen want to meet you.

HARE. What a red face she has. And where did she get those tweeds?

NONESUCH. Hsh, Hare, hsh.

TORY TRUTH. Just a moment, gentlemen; this shooting-stick's a bit wonky. Jolly unfair, you know; Patience can sit on a monument but all I have—and I *am* Truth after all—

HARE. You *are* Truth after all?

TORY TRUTH. Yes—and before all. I have my feet on the earth. The Good Earth, my friends.

NONESUCH (*sotto voce*). Yes—and the Large Feet.

TORY TRUTH. Well . . . what do you want to know?

HARE. We want to know all about you. Is it true that your motto is Back to the Land?

TORY TRUTH. Back to it? I've never left it! Ha! Ha! Ha! You don't catch me, my dear sir, going anywhere near a city. I just don't recognise cities.

HARE. But you must! A city's a fact.

TORY TRUTH. Nothing's a fact unless I choose to admit it. Why, you wouldn't pretend that the Industrial Revolution—

NONESUCH. That was a fact, surely?

TORY TRUTH. Fiddlesticks! As far as I am concerned, it never happened. Nor did Queen Anne's death. Nor did the present Government.

HARE AND NONESUCH. But . . . but . . . .

TORY TRUTH. No, I am Truth. I *know*. Nothing changes. This is the Good Earth. There will always be strapping squires like the Colonel here—

COLONEL. Thank you, madam.

TORY TRUTH. There will always be happy peasants like . . . like . . . Ahoy there, Hodge, come here! Now then, Hodge, show these people how happy you are.

HODGE (*quavering with misery*). Oh, ma'am, it be bitter cold today.

TORY TRUTH. He loves the cold, he loves it.

HODGE. Ah—if I could only get a bellyful of bread—and excuse me, Colonel, touching my forelock, sir, but if you could see your way to repair my roof—

COLONEL. For the thousandth time, Hodge, No! Haven't you heard I'm . . . er . . . bankrupt?

TORY TRUTH. You see. There will always be well set-up squires like the Colonel, there will always be laughing children of

Nature like Hodge, there will always be ten million wireworms per acre, there will always be well-kept fences and (*glamorously*) shining boards saying Trespassers Prosecuted.

HODGE. Ah, that reminds me, that be what I come about. Begging your pardon, Colonel, it bain't my fault none of it, 'twas that there gap in fence . . . .

COLONEL. Well?

HODGE. There be trespassers got in.

COLONEL. Trespassers!

HODGE. Aye, sir. They be holding a party 'tother side of pheasant house.

COLONEL. A party, man?

HODGE. Ah, a party. And what be more, they be playin' about with red rags—I'm afeared old bull may see un.

COLONEL. Well, upon my soul—Where the devil's the gamekeeper?

HODGE. They liquidated him, sir.

COLONEL. They what?

HODGE. He be liquidated, he be.

COLONEL. Oh drunk again, you mean? All right, shoulder guns.

TORY TRUTH. Shoulder shooting sticks. March!

HARE (*gaily*). Come on, Nonesuch. How I enjoy a party. I went to one once in summer under a tree. There was a dormouse there and a young lady whose name, I think, was Alicia . . . .

(*His voice dies away, giving place to a Marxist orchestra.*)

MARXIST. Silence, orchestral shock-troops!

(*The orchestra stops.*)

MARXIST. Comrades! What do I see advancing?

COMRADES. The enemy, comrade.

MARXIST. Correct. What do we do with them?

COMRADES. Shoot them.

MARXIST. Correct. Where is the wall?

1ST COMRADE. What wall, comrade?

MARXIST. The wall to put them up against

2ND COMRADE. There ain't no wall here, comrade.

MARXIST. In that case, comrades, build one.

3RD COMRADE. But they're almost on us, comrade.

MARXIST. Build one, I said. This is a Five Second Plan. One!

COMRADES. One!

MARXIST. Two!

COMRADES. Two!

MARXIST. Three!

COMRADES. Three!

MARXIST. Four!

COMRADES. Four!

MARXIST. Five!

COMRADES. Five!

COLONEL. Hey you! What are you all up to?

MARXIST. What right have you to ask?

COLONEL. I am the landlord.

(Grr! Grr!)

MARXIST. To the wall with him, comrades. Fire!

(Firing on percussion.)

MARXIST. And who are you?

HODGE. I be Hodge.

MARXIST. The Common Man?

HODGE. Oh *I* bain't common, I—

MARXIST. A kulak, eh?

(Grr! Grr!)

MARXIST. To the wall with him, comrades. Fire!

(Firing on percussion—bigger.)

MARXIST. Woman! Who are you?

TORY TRUTH. I am Truth.

(GRR! GRR!)

MARXIST. To the wall with her, comrades. Fire!

(Firing on percussion—biggest.)

MARXIST. And you?

NONESUCH. As a matter of fact I'm—

MARXIST. No, you. The man with the long ears.

HARE. The hare with the long ears.

MARXIST. A hare?

HARE. Yes, comrade. A Marx hare.

MARXIST. Indeed? So you've come to join our party?

HARE. Exactly. Is there any vodka left?

MARXIST. Time enough for vodka. See this line?

HARE. Yes. Rather narrow, isn't it?

MARXIST. You walk along it, comrade. We'll soon see if you've got a sense of direction.

HARE. But why? I've not been drinking.

MARXIST. No—but you may have been thinking.

NONESUCH. No, no, old boy, he's not.

MARXIST. Nobody asked you. Get your paws on that line. Now then. Forward!

HARE. Cross your fingers, Nonesuch . . . .

(*Music takes him on his tortuous course; he pants and grunts in the effort to keep his balance.*)

HARE. Now . . . keep straight, keep straight, keep steady . . . . Left . . . left . . . . Oh, this is narrow . . . . There!

(*The music ends; he has walked the line.*)

MARXIST. You're not through yet. Now do the same thing backwards.

HARE. Cross your legs, Nonesuch . . . . Now.

(*Music as before.*)

HARE. Straight . . . straight . . . steady . . . Left . . . . Left . . . . There!

(*The music ends.*)

NONESUCH. Lucky he's got four left feet.

MARXIST. Very good, comrade. Sit down. Have a cup of tea.

HARE. No vodka?

MARXIST. Certainly not. You're not a commissar yet.

(*Bells are heard in the distance.*)

NONESUCH. What's that?

MARXIST. That is the knell of private property.

HARE. At last! The expropriators are being expropriated.

MARXIST. That's right. Seems you're a well-read hare.

HARE. A well-*red* hare—Ha! Ha! Yes, *I* know the laws of historical necessity.

MARXIST. Good. Have some bread. Tell us more.

HARE. More? Let me see. It is not the consciousness of hares that determines their existence, but on the contrary their social existence determines their consciousness.

(*The comrades cheer.*)

MARXIST. Well done, comrade. Have some marge on it.

HARE. Thank you. Thank you very much.

MARXIST. Comrade; you are qualified now to behold the naked Truth.

HARE. The naked . . . ?

NONESUCH. He never bargained for that, old boy.

MARXIST. Truth is naked or nothing. Truth is ruthless. She can change the future—and she can change the past.

HARE. How can she change the past?

MARXIST. Don't talk like a bourgeois; how do you think? By tearing out pages from the history books.

A COMRADE. That's right.

MARXIST. Comrades, 'shun. She approaches.

(*The orchestra renders an advancing tank.*)

NONESUCH. In a tank, eh? Look out for your paws, Hare.

(*The music—the tank—stops. The comrades chant in unison:*)

COMRADES. We want Truth. We want Truth. We want Truth. T—R—U—T—H—TRUTH!

(*A rousing cheer. In the awkward gap which follows the Hare makes his faux pas.*)

HARE (*plaintively*). But she's not naked.

MARXIST. What's that you said?

HARE. Well maybe she is but I mean in that Marx Four tank—

only her head peeping out of the turret, you know—well, *I* wouldn't call that naked.

(*GRR! GRR!*)

MARXIST. Comrades! Take him to the wall. Liquidate this hare. He's a Trotskyist.

COMRADES. Aye, aye, comrade. Yah, you filthy beast!

(*Hubbub as they bundle him off. He has to raise his voice.*)

HARE. All right, all right; I'm not the first of my family to be shot. Put me against the wall; I have nothing to lose but my brains. And you, Truth, hail and Farewell—

COMRADES. Move along there, move along.

MARXIST. Flat against the wall with him. Haul him up by the ears. Now then, comrades. Slope Arms! . . . Standing Load! . . . Aim—

NONESUCH. Stop, comrades, stop!

MARXIST. What is it?

NONESUCH. Comrades, we all want a free, a classless—perhaps even a hareless—society.

(*Murmurs of approval.*)

NONESUCH. But before you liquidate my friend here, why not attempt a cure? Liquidation is fine but solidification is better.

MARXIST. And what is solidification?

NONESUCH. Comrade, I am surprised at you. (*Rattling it off.*) Solidification is a process of materialistic determinism which by the laws of the dialectic is bound to result in solidarity. And you all know what I mean by solidarity?

COMRADES (*absolutely synchronised*). We do, comrade, we do.

NONESUCH. There you are, you see.

MARXIST. But what sort of cure do you propose? How can you solidify this animal?

NONESUCH. Well, at the moment he's . . . er . . . volatile. We could cure that by sending him to an analyst.

MARXIST (*suspiciously*). You don't mean a psycho-analyst?

NONESUCH. Well, er, yes—why not?

MARXIST. We do not believe in the psych.

NONESUCH. Quite right, old boy—But you know what day this is?

MARXIST. It is the Day of Proletarian Enlightenment—(*cheers*)—a flag in every fist and a tractor in every home.

(*Bigger cheers.*)

NONESUCH. Of course it is, but it's also—jump, Hare, jump—it's also the First of April.

(*The orchestra renders the jump and the race which follows; the angry cries of Stop are left behind; the music lands the Hare and Nonesuch in safety.*)

HARE (*breathless*). Oh what a race. Nonesuch! How did you keep up with me? After all I'm a hare.

NONESUCH (*breathless*). Well . . . after all I'm an agent. But you look as tired as I am. What about a spot of shut-eye?

HARE. Good idea.

(*He yawns; the orchestra takes over with a lullaby.*)

ANALYST (*with a Central European accent*). That is right. Close your eyes, Mr. Hare.

HARE (*starting*). Who're you?

ANALYST. I am your analyst.

HARE. But . . . but . . . but I—

NONESUCH. Excuse me, sir; I never meant that seriously.

ANALYST. Leave the meaning to me. We draw no distinction in psychology between what is called serious—

NONESUCH. Yes, sir, I see your point but I only said it as a ruse; the boys were going to shoot him. He doesn't need to be analysed.

ANALYST. Everyone needs to be analysed. Lie back, Mr. Hare; this will take several years.

HARE. I cannot spare several years. I am in search of Truth.

ANALYST (*archly*). Then you've come to the right shop. You know where Truth resides?

HARE. Not yet. I've been all over the country but—

ANALYST. Foolish Hare, foolish Hare. Truth resides in your own Unconscious.
Do you ever dream, my friend?

NONESUCH. Does he ever not?

ANALYST. Do not interrupt please. I will like it if you look the other way.

NONESUCH. I will like it too. Call me when you're through, Hare.

ANALYST. Now, Mr. Hare. By dreams we come at the truth. Now. What is it most you dream?

HARE. Ah, most I dream I am up in the moon—

ANALYST. Good, good.

HARE. With a butterfly net, you know—

ANALYST. I know. You catch the butterflies.

HARE. No, no, I catch the humming-birds. But that's not my strangest dream. Sometimes I dream I'm a man in the British Museum Reading Room.

ANALYST. You read the book?

HARE. Of course not; I have the bath. With lots of bath salts in it.

ANALYST. So? What kind of bath salts please?

HARE. Oh just the usual. Verbena, gardenia, amnesia, euthanasia—

ANALYST. So? Where do you buy these bath salts?

HARE. Black Market of course. Black Market.

ANALYST. Good. Give me the address please. Now where is my hat?

HARE. But—!

ANALYST. I have not for years bath salts. But make please haste. The address!

HARE. But there isn't any address. I told you this was a dream.

ANALYST. A dream! Damn all dreams! I was thinking you tell me the truth.

HARE. But you said that by dreams we come at the truth.

ANALYST. Ach! There is the door, Mr. Hare. You are not good for analysis.

NONESUCH. And it's not good for him. Come on, Hare, let's hop it.

HARE. Goodbye, Mr. Analyst. Have a nice bath.

(The door bangs.)

ANALYST (*furious*). So? He leaves me holding the bath-tub. I shall no more try this hare treatment. No more hares! No!

(A pause; his tone changes to controlled malevolence.)

He likes the bath? Good; let him go and get drowned. I wish for him now to go to that place which in all the world makes the hare most wet. Where is my atlas? So. Now where does it tell me the rainfall?

('The Harp that Once' seeps in on an ocarina.)

HARE. Nonesuch! What's that music?

NONESUCH. Sounds like the 'Harp that Once'.

HARE. The harp that once? Once what?

NONESUCH. The Harp that Once and never got over it. Tara's Halls, sir, Tara's Halls.

HARE. I've never been to Tara's Halls. Might we find my Lady Truth there?

NONESUCH. We might—but we won't find any halls.

HARE. No matter. Truth looks fairer in the open air.

NONESUCH. In the rain, you mean. O.K. Next stop, Tara.

(The tune ends, giving place to heavy rain.)

HARE. What a very wet place.

NONESUCH. What a very wet man.

HARE. Who?

NONESUCH. That chap there who's lost his trousers.

GAEL. Is it me has lost me trousers? The ignorance of yez! This is me saffron kilt.

NONESUCH. But you're soaking, old man. You ought to go home and change.

GAEL. Ach, I don't fancy the changes. And who minds soakin' anyway?

HARE. But he's right. You ought to go home.

GAEL. Sure this is me home—here on the sod of Tara. Me ancestors lie underneath it.

NONESUCH. You'll lie underneath it too if you stand out here in the rain.

GAEL. Rain? So ye call this rain!

(*He sneezes violently.*)

GAEL. I can see ye're English—the pair of yez.

HARE. English? Of course we're English.

GAEL. Ah poor fellows. There was nothing good ever come out of England. Sure *I* wouldn't use anything that was English.

NONESUCH. Except the language.

GAEL. Ah I only use that when I'm talkin' to black foreigners. When I'm here by meself I talk to meself in the Gaelic.

HARE. And do you understand yourself?

GAEL. I do. At times I do. There's great truth in the Gaelic.

HARE. Truth!

GAEL. Great and beautiful truth.

HARE. Nonesuch, we're on the track! Truth, sir, you say—Truth is a beautiful woman?

GAEL. She is, indeed she is. I know her well.

HARE. But she only speaks Gaelic, you say?

GAEL. What else would she speak? Isn't her proper name not Truth at all.

HARE. No? What *is* her name then?

GAEL. Cathleen ni Houlihan.

HARE. Cathleen ni—Nonesuch, make a note of that. And I must learn Gaelic. Buy me a grammar, Nonesuch.

GAEL. Why are ye wantin' a grammar?

HARE. Because I must speak with this lady. You're sure that she knows no English?

GAEL. Know English, is it? May the Round Towers turn square! Would she soil her delicate ears and be twistin' her beautiful mouth and pollutin' her pure green blood with a heathen language like that?

Whisht—that's her now in the shawl. Takin' up her entrenched position over the graves of the kings. She'll be singin' now, so keep quiet . . . .

HARE. Singing in Gaelic?

GAEL. Amn't I after tellin' ye—

(*He is cut off by a soprano singing in a cockney accent.*)

SOPRANO. The blue moon is setting beyond the red pylon
But south of the Border the whisky flows free

NONESUCH. Gaelic?

SOPRANO. With all the colleens wearing stockings of nylon
And Father O'Flynn rolling down to the sea—

HARE. But surely she's singing in English?

SOPRANO. And ock! the dear mem'ries they still linger on
Of Cuchullain and Guinness and Oscar and Conn.

GAEL (*outraged*). Stop! Stop! . . .

SOPRANO. With a carp on the harp and a salmon in the Shannon
And the Poor Old Woman with the sorrows in her shawl

GAEL. Put on the other record! . . .

SOPRANO. An' meself on the shelf and King Billy on his filly—
Oh hadn't we the sophistree on Tuesday in the House?

(*The orchestra alone while the Gael fumes.*)

GAEL. Change that record or I'll smash ye . . . I'm warnin' ye now; I'll smash ye.

SOPRANO. For Ock! the dear mem'ries—(*first smash but the song is obstinate*) they still linger on

(*The Gael does his second smash, shouting 'Take that!' The soprano's voice cracks on the word 'on'.*)

'ANNOUNCER.' Owing to a technical hitch we return you now to the studio. The March Hare will be with us in a moment. He is crossing from Ireland on the Home Service wave-length.

(*Whispering and crackling of scripts.*)

'ANNOUNCER.' I'm sorry; I'll read that again. The March Hare will *not* be with us in a moment. He has boarded a very high frequency wave-length unobtainable on any wireless set. That is the end of the news.

(Out of the violet distance comes a Yogi shanty-spiritual.)

DISCIPLES. Om—Om—Yogi!
Om—Om—Swami!
Om—Om—Yogi!
Breathe, boys, breathe!

(This is repeated till we have joined the congregation. It ends loud.)

YOGI (*in a high, mystical quasi-oriental monotone*). Thank you, my children. We will now contemplate until April the First next year. I myself during this period shall not eat, speak or sleep—

NONESUCH (*calling from below*). Excuse me, sir!

YOGI (*from above*). Who are you?

HARE. Pilgrims in search of Truth. If you would kindly descend that rope—

YOGI. I may not descend to your level. You can speak to me from there.

HARE. Well, it's rather a strain on the voice but—Are you a Yogi, sir?

YOGI. I am a neo-Yogi. Whatever I am I am. Whatever I am not I am.

NONESUCH (*sotto voce*). Simple. Simple.

HARE. Why do you sit up there at the top of that rope?

YOGI. Why not?

HARE. Yes, quite—but what's the rope fastened to?

YOGI. Nothing.

HARE. Nothing!

YOGI. Which is the same as everything.
You two are in time, aren't you?

HARE. In time for what?

YOGI. I am above time. This is the higher level of existence.

HARE. And where is Truth?

YOGI. Truth is up here beside me.

HARE. I can't see her.

YOGI. You wouldn't. You are blinded by your own personality.

HARE. But how can I reach her?

YOGI. By climbing up this rope.

HARE. I can't do that.

YOGI. No, you can't. Please go away. You smell.

HARE. I don't.

YOGI. You do. You smell of personality. *I* am above personality.

NONESUCH. You're above yourself, cock.

YOGI. Yes. I am above myself.

NONESUCH. Oh come on, Hare, let's go.

HARE. Go? I have been insulted. Also I have been challenged. Do you think I could climb that rope?

NONESUCH. No.

HARE. Nor do I. But never let it be said that the March Hare—I shall take a ten yards run.

NONESUCH. Make it twenty.

HARE. I'll make it twenty-five. Now then, One—Two—Three!

(*The orchestra pulls; down comes rope, Yogi and all.*)

YOGI (*lapsing into cockney*). You little meddling rodent! You've pulled the whole thing down.

NONESUCH. Well, well, well—money for old rope.

HARE. A thousand apologies, sir. I hope you're not hurt?

YOGI. A neo-Yogi cannot be hurt.

NONESUCH. Then what are you rubbing your shin for?

YOGI. I am *not* rubbing my—

HARE. Of course you're not. Now let's put up this rope again.

YOGI. We can't.

HARE. Why not?

YOGI (*recovering his manner*). I decline to answer that question.

NONESUCH. He means the stage carpenter's gone.

YOGI. What I mean I mean. What I do not mean I mean. (*lapsing again.*) You might have known that rope wouldn't bear two of us.

HARE. But I thought you said—

(*The Yogi begins his comeback in cockney, then starts again at the beginning of the sentence.*)

YOGI. What I have said is the same as what I have not said. Has either of you seen a paper parcel?

LITTLE BIT OF PAPER. Here am I, just a little bit of paper, wrapping up sandwiches, ham and spam—

NONESUCH. Aha!

YOGI (*snatching*). Give me those; they're mine.

NONESUCH. He's off. And never thanked me. Untidy chap, too, throwing that paper on the ground.

LITTLE BIT OF PAPER. Pick me up, pick me up; I can help you, I can help you; thank you very much—now read me, read me—

NONESUCH. Cover of a journal—'Science for All'—

LITTLE BIT OF PAPER. That's right—read me, read me—P.T.O. for all the gossip—M. & B. for colds and 'flu—

NONESUCH. The B.M.A. for L.S.D.—

LITTLE BIT OF PAPER. The Chemical Age, (*coyly*) a Note on Manure—The Plastic Age, a Hint on Housing—The Atomic Age, the Truth about Voltage—

HARE. The *Truth* about—

LITTLE BIT OF PAPER. Science owns the Door to the Future! Ring the Bell and the Door will Open!

HARE. Nonesuch! Ring the bell, please.

(*A cranky doorbell tinkles. A door opens. A maid.*)

MAID (*forbiddingly*). Yes?

NONESUCH. The Scientist in?

MAID. Yes—but he's not to be disturbed.

NONESUCH. Working?

MAID. He's splitting something. What he calls nuclear fission.

HARE. I don't care. I must see him.

(*He shouts past her.*)

Scientist! Scientist! Where are you?

SCIENTIST (*silkily; he is beside them*). Here I am.

HARE. I'm afraid you're very busy—

SCIENTIST. I'm always very busy. Looking for Truth.

HARE. But that's what I've come about! I'm looking for her too.

SCIENTIST. *Her? It*, my dear sir. Metaphors are unsound.

HARE. But I'm going to marry it—her, I mean.

SCIENTIST. Tck! Tck! Tck! Metaphors are unsound. If you use them too much, you'll get into heavy water. Now, gentlemen, if you don't mind coming into my lab—

(*A door opens—cumbrously. When Nonesuch speaks his voice has a quite new resonance.*)

NONESUCH. Lab? This looks like the Albert Hall!

SCIENTIST (*gently*). It *is* the Albert Hall. I've hired it for my performance on the cyclotron.

HARE. And this is where you look for Truth?

SCIENTIST. This is where Truth will appear.

HARE. Out of these machines?

SCIENTIST. Out of these machines, as you call them.

NONESUCH. See your mistake, Hare? None of the other boys had a decent plant.

Do you know, sir? Mr. Hare here and I have spent this whole day consulting experts on Truth.

SCIENTIST. There *are* no experts. Except yours truly. You've heard of atomic energy?

NONESUCH. Well . . . we've heard it mentioned.

SCIENTIST. Only mentioned? Dear me, the public are slow in the uptake. Of course the uranium atom was only a modest beginning. But atomic energy is truth and I hope to get more and more of it. If now I were to split some other kind of atom—

HARE. A hare for example?

SCIENTIST. A hair!

HARE. Me.

SCIENTIST. Oh very good joke, sir; I always enjoy a pun.

HARE. It isn't a pun, sir; it is a proposition.

SCIENTIST. Really? But have you any reason to suppose that *you* could release much energy?

HARE. I am the March Hare. Reason to suppose—! Watch me.

(*The orchestra renders him jumping.*)

NONESUCH. There he goes. Clean into the Upper Gallery.

SCIENTIST. Astonishing; quite astonishing.

NONESUCH. He comes of a family of athletes. They're all of them running at Aintree on Friday, you know.

SCIENTIST. Really? This interests me exceedingly. Supposing accepted your friend as a subject for nuclear fission—

NONESUCH. Nuclear what—

SCIENTIST. Ah, here he is, coming back again.

(*The orchestra brings the Hare down.*)

NONESUCH. Nice jumping, Hare, nice jumping.

HARE. I always land on my paws.

SCIENTIST. Mr. Hare, let me congratulate you. You *are* a source of energy. (*Wooingly*) I would very much like to try a small experiment on you.

HARE. An experiment?

SCIENTIST. Yes. For the sake of Truth.

HARE. For *her* sake I will do anything.

SCIENTIST. I should warn you, there is a very slight risk—

HARE. Only a slight risk? Why, for the sake of that beautiful lady—

NONESUCH. Look here, Hare, old leveret—

HARE. Electric hares we have heard of; *I* shall be the first Atomic Hare!
I have made up my mind. Let's go.

SCIENTIST. There is no need to go. Here is the cyclotron before you. Now please take your place in this pill-box. Now . . . we just screw you in . . . .

(*The Hare grunts during this.*)

So. Now when I've closed this lid we'll begin the bombardment.

NONESUCH (*startled*). Bombardment?

SCIENTIST (*gloatingly*). Ten million volts, my dear sir. Ready, Mr. Hare?

HARE. Close that lid. When this operation is over, may I see Truth face to face?

SCIENTIST. Truth has no face. Metaphors, as I said, are—

HARE. No face? Then let me out!

SCIENTIST. Oh no you don't.

(*Music closes the lid.*)

SCIENTIST. Atomic Energy Team! Stand by for action. Target for bombardment is the March Hare. Give him the works. Fission!

(*Music gives him the works.*)

SCIENTIST. Fine. Accelerate! . . . Accelerate!

(*The music accelerates and leads into the Chorus: 'The Old March Hare he ain't what he used to be, Only an hour ago!' The job is done.*)

SCIENTIST. You see? Now we open the lid.

(*As the lid opens, two snarling voices are heard.*)

NONESUCH. Good Lord, there are two of him now.

SCIENTIST. Nuclear fission, my friend. But they're both alive—and energetic, you'll find.
Come on, you two, climb out.

1ST HARE. No, you don't, you cad.

2ND HARE. I saw her first.

1ST HARE. Truth! She's mine.

2ND HARE. She's not, she's mine. My bride!

1ST HARE. Is she? We'll see about that.

2ND HARE. Take your paws off me.

(*They squeal and growl at each other.*)

NONESUCH. Hare! Hare, old boy.

SCIENTIST. Be accurate. They're plural.

NONESUCH. Hares, old boys. Stop it!

1ST HARE. Stop it, indeed!

2ND HARE. You keep out of this, Nonesuch.
Take that, you filthy rodent!

1ST HARE. Rodent yourself! Wait till I get my teeth in you.

2ND HARE. Ow!
Two can play at that game.

1ST HARE. Ow!

(*Both Hares scream and scuffle.*)

SCIENTIST (*delighted*). What energy, what energy! But don't let's waste it. Help me to hold them apart.
Come, come, gentlemen . . . .

(*Nonesuch seconds him. The animal noises stop.*)

SCIENTIST. There!
And have you seen Truth, my friends?

BOTH HARES. I have.

SCIENTIST. But she has no face?

BOTH HARES. She *has* a face.

1ST HARE. There! Can't you see it! Look up.

2ND HARE. It fills the Albert Hall.

NONESUCH (*sotto voce*). More than the Vigilantes could.

1ST HARE. Beautiful, Nonesuch, beautiful. My one and only bride!

2ND HARE. *Your* one and only? Beast!

1ST HARE. Beast? Put up your paws!

NONESUCH. Now, now, boys, don't start all that again. There's two of you and there's only one of Truth.

(*This releases the echoes.*)

TORY TRUTH. But *I* am Truth.

JOURNALISTS' TRUTH. *I* am Truth.

POETIC TRUTH. *I* am Truth.

NONESUCH. Seem to be some ghosts around today.

SCIENTIST. Oh the Albert Hall is like that.

TORY TRUTH. It is. It never changes.

HARE. Silence! You're liquidated.

JOURNALISTS' TRUTH. Yeah—but what about me?

POETIC TRUTH. And me? You offered your paw to *me*.

ANALYST. Truth is in your Unconscious.

MARXIST. Truth is what we decide at our next meeting.

YOGI. Truth is at the top of a rope.

GAEL. Where's that record they put on back to front?

PHOTOGRAPHER. Where's that photo? I think I'll touch it up now.

HARE. Where is this! Where is that! Silence, all of you. Where is the Face?

SCIENTIST (*smugly*). Has it gone?

HARE. It was here just now. Up here above us floating under the roof. But now it's vanished—And what's that thing in its place?

SCIENTIST. That? That's a diagram. One of my own.

HARE. So you have fooled me too.

SCIENTIST (*still cooing*). Well . . . it's April the First.

(*The orchestra begins Alleluia.*)

HARE. One moment please!

(*The orchestra obliges him and stops.*)

HARE. One moment please. Then you can have your finale.

(*This releases a hive of ringing shouts.*)

GAEL. We don't want any finallies. Up the rebels!

ANALYST. Up the Oedipus Complex!

TORY TRUTH. Up the Upper Ten!

MARXIST. Up the Inevitability of History!

JOE. Up the Circulation of the Late Night Final!

YOGI. Up the Immanent and Transcendent Rope!

SCIENTIST. Up the New Era of Atomic Energy!

POETIC TRUTH. Up the Beautiful Ineffectual Angel who is older than the rocks on which she sits and—

HARE. Up the Garden Path! April Fools all of you.

(*The Truths and the Experts hiss.*)

HARE. Why do you hiss? Don't you know what day this is? I, the March Hare, I also have been fooled. But I can survive. Can you?

Whatever I am, I am not so narrow as some; a hare may have

curious eyes but he wears no blinkers. I have not won my bride—but I have not married a stuffed one. And, if it is April the First, it is also Spring. The daffodils blow their trumpets, there is green fire in the hedge-rows, there is even a new note in the ring of the office telephone. It is your Spring—but it is also mine. Fetch me my springboard, Nonesuch.

Ladies and gentlemen, I am about to take off. Follow me if you dare. Hail and Farewell. I salute you!

(The orchestra plays the finale on the Alleluia theme—When it has finished the Announcer speaks in the 'dead' studio.)

ANNOUNCER. You have just heard Salute to—Salute to—Salute to—

SWEET VOICE. Salute to the Public?

ANNOUNCER. Quite so.

NOTES

N 2

NOTES

The Dark Tower

Page 23. *Roland as a boy* was, in the broadcast, brilliantly doubled by Cyril Cusack.

Page 28. *The tolling bell*, instead of being done by percussion alone, was reinforced and made ultra-suggestive by strings. Apart from percussion and one trumpet (reserved for the Challenge Call) Benjamin Britten confined himself in this programme to an orchestra of twenty-six strings from which he got the most varied and astonishing effects.

Page 29. *The Child of Stone* puzzled many listeners. The Mother in bearing so many children only to send them to their death, can be thought of as thereby bearing a series of deaths. So her logical last child is stone—her own death. This motif has an echo in the stone in the ring.

Page 30. *The Verbal Transition* from one scene to another is controlled from the panel and need not seem either abrupt or confusing. It not only makes a change from the musical transition but has certain positive advantages; e.g. as here, irony.

Page 38. *The Soak* I should have called Solipsist if that word were known to the public. His alcoholism is an effect rather than a cause. Robert Farquharson wonderfully achieved the right leer in the voice and the dream-like sinister undertones.

Page 41. *'I'm dreaming you'* is a famous stumper for reason. Compare *Alice Through the Looking Glass*, the episode of Tweedledee and the Red King:

' "And if he left off dreaming about you, where do you suppose you'd be?"

"Where I am now, of course," said Alice.

"Not you!" Tweedledee retorted contemptuously. "You'd be nowhere. Why, you're only a sort of thing in his dream!" '

Page 42. *The Stentorian Voice* butting in here changes the scene with the speed of a dream. Radio, like dreams, having no set stage, can disregard spatial conventions.

Page 47. '*The sea today*': this covers a number of days. The developing false idyl of Roland and Neaera is intercut with the voices of people playing tombola—always the same again. The idyl also is merely killing time.

Page 57. *The Mirage Sequence* needed a great deal of rehearsal but the stunt came off.

Page 63. *The Final Decision* may, I think, be too abrupt for a listener—though in life such a complex psychological conflict can, of course, resolve itself abruptly.

Page 64. *The Last Scene* is naturally the nearest to Browning. Compare:

> 'Not see? because of night perhaps?—why day
> Came back again for that! before it left,
> The dying sunset kindled through a cleft:
> The hills, like giants at a hunting, lay,
> Chin upon hand, to see the game at bay,—
> "Now stab and end the creature—to the heft!"
>
> Not hear? when noise was everywhere! it tolled
> Increasing like a bell. Names in my ears
> Of all the lost adventurers my peers . . .'.

Sunbeams in his Hat

Acknowledgment is made to Constance Garnett from whose translations of Tchehov's plays I have quoted.

Page 73. *Tchehov died* of consumption at Badenweiler on July 2nd, 1904, at the age of forty-four; there is an account of this last day (the day which sets my programme) by his wife Olga Knipper. In his last letter to his sister, dated June 28th, he had complained both of the heat in Badenweiler and of the German lack of taste in dress, etc., and had played with the idea of escaping to Odessa by steamer from Trieste. In earlier letters he had complained of German 'peace and order' and of the 'very expensive but talentless band' that played in the garden.

Page 78. *The visit to Sahalin* happened in 1890. Tchehov, who chose this island as a place 'where colonization by convicts can be studied', afterwards wrote a book about it which is said to have influenced the authorities to bring in some reforms. I stressed this Sahalin mission because it illustrates Tchehov's 'social consciousness'.

Page 80. *The incident of the Boy* is recorded in a letter to A. F. Koni.

Page 84. *Faites vos jeux*: I used Offenbach's can-can—inappropriate to the tempo of Monte Carlo, but right, I thought, for Tchehov's mood.

Page 86. *The Seagull* was first produced in 1896 in Petersburg, where it failed miserably. Tchehov wrote to his brother: 'The moral is: I must not write plays.'

Page 89. *Tolstoy and Gorki* often had such arguments in Tchehov's presence, as admitted by Gorki himself.

Page 91. '*Vaudeville*': Tchehov's own word for it.

Page 92. *Stanislavsky* I left uncharacterised on purpose. This was not the moment to introduce such a personality.

Page 95. *The Clock* is, I think now, rather a creaking device.

Page 95. *The River*: Tchehov wrote in a letter: 'When the quilt slides from my body during the night, I begin to dream of huge, slippery stones, cold autumn waters, naked banks,—all this vaguely, as in a fog, without a bit of blue sky showing; in melancholy and depression I gaze on the stones and feel, for some reason, the inevitability of crossing a deep river.'

THE NOSEBAG.

Page 101. *The best English version* of this story is *The Soldier and Death* by Arthur Ransome; I had not however come across it when I wrote my script.

Notes

Page 104. *The Third Beggar* is in some versions, though not in Mr. Ransome's, identified with Christ. Hence the line 'Do you not know who I am?' Without using a Narrator I could not be more explicit.

Page 104. *The nosebag* is by Mr. Ransome called a 'sack'—no doubt a more correct translation. But the word 'nosebag' sticks more.

Page 107. *The music stops* so aptly because it is an actor. Compare in *Salute to All Fools* the waltz at the Charity Ball.

Page 109. *The bestial noises* of the devils were achieved by a mixture of discs on the turn-tables and voices in the studio; my key disc was a recording of jabbering apes.

Page 111. *The square brackets*, here and later, denote cuts which I had to make in the broadcast merely for lack of time.

Page 113. *No bones in the palace*: in the narrative versions the Soldier is still in the palace when the Tsar sends round to investigate. This is one of several changes dictated by dramatic economy.

Page 114. *The clanging in the smithy* could have been rendered either by a spot effect in the studio or by a gramophone record. We had to decide whether to be realistic; these were corporeal devils and what the hammers would strike would be not the anvil but their bodies. In the end I disregarded realism and plumped for a ringing noise. The records of real smithies being too unpoetic, I used a recorded bell-bird.

Page 120. *The cut in the broadcast* here was very regrettable as the two earlier sickbeds were needed in order to 'build' to the Tsar's. The rigid time-limit of B.B.C. programmes has often undone things so.

Page 123. *The voice of Death* would be out of most actresses' compass. Miss Gladys Young attained it. While this programme was meant to be fun, I had no intention that 'Death' should be merely funny. She had to be frightening—and, in a way, pathetic.

Page 131. *The Gates of Paradise* more than anything else would have been strengthened by specially written music.

Notes

Page 132. *The War Theme* was my own interpolation; the traditional version ends less committally—'For all I know he may be living yet.' I added this piece of homage to the moujik because of what was happening as I wrote—at the beginning of 1944. This lays me open to the two charges of sentimentality and dramatic incongruity. The latter I deny; that the Soldier should go to war again and that the Landlord should toast Mother Russia are no more out of key than the characterisation of Death (see above). As for sentimentality (and the Mother Russia theme has nothing to do with the policy of the Soviet Union) I greatly admired and admire the courage of the Russian soldier; this story after all was about the same type of man and it was the same type of man who made this story.

The March Hare Resigns

Page 139. '*Not yet All Fools' Day*': When I suggested this programme, I meant it for April 1st, 1945, but, as this was discovered to be Easter Day, the date had to be changed.

Page 139. '*The paws of the March Hare*': a talking animal is in pantomime a mere buffoon. To 'see' him as a character, you must not see him. The Dog in *The Witch of Edmonton* must, I imagine, be silly on the stage—but he *would* be 'radiogenic'.

Page 139. '*Daffodils over the microphone*': we did have some over the microphone.

Page 139. '*The pitch was sticky*': both the March Hare programmesare full of puns and other plays upon words. These can be very offensive if they are emphasised. My principle in producing is to have them thrown in quickly and matter-of-factly and leave it to the listener to catch it or miss it.

Page 141. *The Public Address Voice* was inspired by the classic example in Baker Street Underground station.

Page 152. *The Safe Hotel*: compare Nathaniel Gubbins. Mr. Gubbins' excellent column in the *Sunday Express* makes a concentrated use of the same brand of salt which the March Hare sprinkles in passing.

Salute to All Fools

Page 170. '*My uncle won the boat race*': up to the day of transmission he had won the hurdles. But Oxford had beaten Cambridge on March 30th.

Page 171. *The Poet* and his Truth are, of course, misrepresentations. I was thinking of a foolish and tiresome kind of poet and a narrow conception of poetry; had I been writing for a highbrow public, I should have been more specific. To quote—or misquote—Shelley and Pater in such a burlesque may be, by some, thought blasphemy. But without some blasphemy where should we be?

Page 183. *The Gael* is hardly a caricature (see any Irish nationalist paper). To those who accuse me of fouling my own doorstep, let me say that I dissociate the language lunacy from the question of Eire's independence; I am glad that she runs her own house but why need she keep the windows shut?

Page 186. *The Neo-Yogi* was inspired not by the East but by California. It was Laidman Browne (who played the part brilliantly) who had the idea of adding an extra facet by making the Yogi a cockney in disguise.

Page 189. *Nuclear fission*: if anyone deplores the burlesque of this serious subject, I hold to what I said about blasphemy.

Page 191. *The Two Hares*, speaking or snarling at once, were achieved by pre-recording Esmé Percy and 'dubbing' together two sets of discs.

Page 194. *Salute to the Public*: some of them rose to it.